FISHING UP NORTH

Stories of Luck and Loss in Alaskan Waters

T0160122

BRAD MATSEN

Alaska Northwest Books®

For Kurt, Kay, Rose, and Michael

First edition published 1998.

Library of Congress Cataloging-in-Publication-Data:
Matsen, Bradford.
    Fishing up North : stories of luck and loss in Alaskan waters / by
Brad Matsen.
        p.   cm.
    ISBN 978-0-88240-896-5
    1. Fisheries—Alaska—Anecdotes. 2. Fishers—Alaska—Anecdotes.
I. Title.
SH222.A4M38   1998
338.3'727'09798—dc21   97-44588
                                                                    CIP

Designers: Elizabeth Watson, Vicki Knapton
Map: Gray Mouse Graphics

Alaska Northwest Books®
An imprint of Graphic Arts Books
P.O. Box 56118
Portland, OR 97238-6118
(503) 254-5591
www.graphicartsbooks.com

Acknowledgments

I am grateful to have been a witness and recorder of some of the events and circumstances of this time. I am especially indebted to the fishermen and others in the fishing community who were so willing to allow me into their lives. Many thanks, also, to my editors and colleagues, John Pappenheimer at the *Alaska Fisherman's Journal*; Jim Fullilove, Chris Cornell, Hugh McKellar, Mike Crowley, and Marydale Abernathy at *National Fisherman*; and Mike Robbins at *Oceans* and *Audubon* for giving me, as fishermen say, a chance. Linda Gunnarson did a fine job of making these stories make sense, and Marlene Blessing, my friend and editor at Alaska Northwest Books, is again part of the great good fortune of my life. As always, my daughter Laara brought me endless inspiration and joy.

Contents

Prelude: Getting Lucky 7
Map 10

1 The Beast of Ugly Seasons   13
KING CRABBING • DUTCH HARBOR, 1981

2 Talking Price and the Cruel Sixteen 25
SALMON GILLNETTING • BRISTOL BAY, 1981

3 The Billion-dollar Bottomfish Dream 47
GROUNDFISH TRAWLING • KODIAK, 1985

4 Kenny and the Council 61
WESTWARD HILTON HOTEL • ANCHORAGE, 1986

5 Flying Fish and the Death of a Plane at Egegik 81
SALMON SETNETTING • BRISTOL BAY, 1985

6 A Beautiful Place to Be 107
SALMON TROLLING • SOUTHEAST ALASKA, 1987

7 Fishing with Modest Ambition 129
CODFISH TRAWLING • KODIAK, 1987

8 Fishing the Flats 147
SALMON GILLNETTING • PRINCE WILLIAM SOUND, 1987

9 The Dream Comes True on the Chain 161
POLLOCK TRAWLING • DUTCH HARBOR, 1988

10 The Resurrection of the *Rebecca B* 177
CODFISH LONGLINING • GULF OF ALASKA, 1989

11 Kelping for Crude 195
THE *EXXON VALDEZ* SPILL • PRINCE WILLIAM SOUND, 1989

12 Derby Days, Sleepless Nights 209
HALIBUT LONGLINING • SOUTHEAST ALASKA, 1992

13 Salmon in the Trees 225
LOGGING THE TONGASS • SOUTHEAST ALASKA, 1999

*Alaska, once again, was a last frontier.
People will continue to fish for a living, but
we all sail on a very different ocean now.*

Prelude

GETTING LUCKY

The good luck that frees a man or woman to fish for a living came to me at midlife when I bought a barely serviceable boat, sailed from my home in Juneau, Alaska, and went salmon trolling. My partner and I did everything wrong, including tying our gear on backward for the first two weeks, but we were euphoric for the whole season and, eventually, even caught enough fish to make it pay. I lasted only two years, though, mostly because the long seasons conflicted with fatherhood and I couldn't take my daughter, Laara, with me. My luck, however, held beyond my time on the grounds.

What you have here is a collection of a dozen stories, originally published between 1980 and 1992, some in slightly different versions, in National Fisherman, the Alaska Fisherman's Journal, Audubon, and Oceans. Together, they are an account of the Alaskan fishing grounds, which crackled with adventure and enterprise during the years after passage of the Magnuson Fishery Conservation and Management Act of 1976, America's chief fisheries law. Until its revision in 1996, the Act clearly stimulated development, but now fisheries everywhere are changing gait from unbridled growth to sustainability. Incredibly, we have reached or exceeded the capacity of many fish stocks to surrender meals to a booming human population.

In 1989, the United Nations Food and Agriculture Organization, in a routine annual report on the world's food supply, shocked everyone whose lives are entwined with the sea, meaning everybody on Earth. After a steady rise from 20 million tons per year just after World War II, the production capacity of the ocean peaked at about 90 million tons in 1988 and then flattened out. The catch has grown no further, despite the fact that the world's fishing nations are pumping about $230 billion a year into the fleets to produce seafood worth about $175 billion. No matter how hard we fish, it appears, the ocean we once thought would keep up with the burgeoning human population's demand for food hollers, "Enough!"

As I traveled and wrote on the Alaskan fishing grounds, it became apparent to me that fishermen were instinctively aware of this shift in our basic perceptions about the sea. By 1985, true environmental coverage began to make its way into the fishing trade papers and magazines, and soon people in fishing communities— particularly in Alaska, where most fish stocks still are quite healthy—were what you might call pretty "green." The fisheries development boom that spanned the 1980s, we all could sense, was the last wave of an infinite ocean crashing onto the shores of the Aleutians, Cook Inlet, Prince William Sound, and the Southeast Alaska archipelago. Alaska, once again, was a last frontier. People will continue to fish for a living, but we all sail on a very different ocean now.

Regardless of the politics, economics, and biological truths that swirl around the business of extracting food from the sea, the people out there with the fleets are just doing what people do. They are ambitious, brave, frightened, rich, poor, confused, and amused, but fishing somehow differentiates them from other streaks of life here at the end of the twentieth century. These accounts of a mere dozen years in the histories of fishing people are a heartbeat in the record of thousands of seasons, but, for better or worse, they did immediately precede our discovery that the ocean is not infinite in its ability to produce food.

The stories in *Fishing Up North* are arranged as I wrote them, in chronological order, covering the major fisheries on the Bering Sea and Gulf of Alaska, with one exception. At the risk of submitting readers to the same tedium as fishermen at meetings, I include out of order a chapter on the workings of the North Pacific Fishery Management Council, the eleven men and women who make the rules for the fisheries off Alaska. I also include a chapter on the *Exxon Valdez* disaster, which delivered a terrible blow to fishermen and, at least momentarily, alerted the industrial world to another variation of the folly of dominion over nature. Throughout this book, any errors of fact or recollection are my own, and I apologize in advance for the inevitable mistakes.

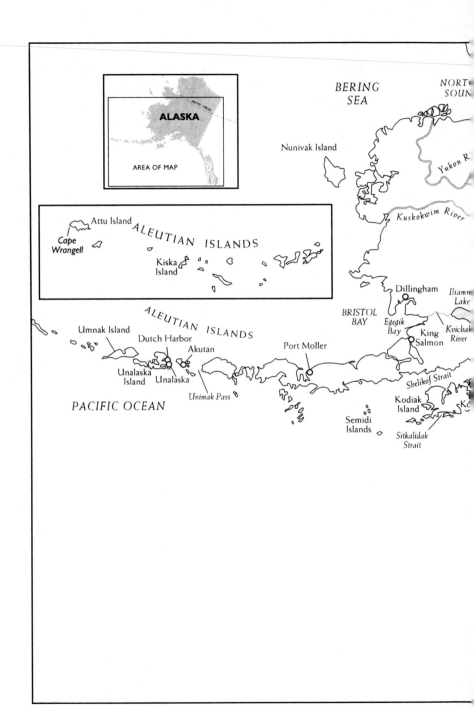

ALASKA

AREA OF MAP

BERING
SEA

NORT
SOUN

Nunivak Island

Yukon R

Kuskokwim River

Attu Island

Cape
Wrangell

ALEUTIAN ISLANDS

Kiska
Island

Dillingham   Iliamn
                  Lake

BRISTOL
BAY   Egegik
           Bay   King   Kvichak
                  Salmon   River

ALEUTIAN ISLANDS

Umnak Island
Dutch Harbor
           Akutan

Port Moller

Unalaska
Island   Unalaska

Unimak Pass

PACIFIC OCEAN

Shelikof Strait

Kodiak
Island   Ko

Semidi
Islands   Sitkalidak
           Strait

ARCTIC CIRCLE

Yukon River

Mount McKinley

A L A S K A

Anchorage

Copper River

Soldotna

Inlet

KENAI
PENINSULA

CHUGACH

Valdez

MTNS

WRANGELL-ST. ELIAS RANGE

chemak
Bay   Resurrection   Cordova
Bay

Prince William
Sound

GULF OF ALASKA

Yakutat

Mt. Fairweather

Fairweather
Grounds

Juneau

PACIFIC OCEAN

Frederick
Sound
Sitka

Petersburg

Southeast
Alaska

Ketchikan

MILES			
0	100	200	300

0	100	200	300
	KILOMETERS		

The Beast of Ugly Seasons

KING CRABBING ▪ DUTCH HARBOR, 1981

We're trying to get used to a few less zeros around here."
— Frank Bohannon, F/V Neahkahnie

"When the going gets weird, the weird turn pro."
— Hunter Thompson

For the first couple of weeks of the Bering Sea king crab season, it made perfect sense, in a twisted sort of way, to just forget that the forecasts said the crab had vanished. After all, it's a little tough to go out into one of the meanest oceans in the world, burn up enough fuel to light Vegas for a year, and run the risk of being maimed or killed unless you think there's a lot of money in it. So during the early going, the wisdom on the radio from the grounds went like this: "The first trip doesn't mean much anyway" . . . "They're all dug down in the mud" . . . "They're here; they're just not feeding" . . . "Somebody's got to be on them."

In Dutch Harbor and Akutan on the Aleutian Chain, packers were going through the usual motions, flying in hundreds of workers at $800 a crack round trip, tuning up the cooking and freezing equipment, and generally hoping that the season wouldn't be all that bad, that the great swarms of crab would again materialize. For five years, the king crab season had been a license to print money for almost everyone who showed up out on the Chain, and it was clear that expectations were going to die hard.

At Pan Alaska Seafoods, the tidy blue-and-white compound on the Unalaska side of Dutch, superintendent Greg Gerhardstein was holding twice-daily sessions known as "radio schedule" when he called around his fleet for scores, parts and supply orders, and delivery times. Assembled in the office with him were his foreman, parts boss, assistants of one sort or another, and, crouched in the corner, the Beast of Ugly Seasons. The first loads were coming in after a full week of fishing, and the outlook wasn't brilliant. The high boat so far had come in with about half a load, and the skip molts and tired crab shot the dead loss way up. But Gerhardstein was hanging in there, and his strong, polite voice reached a couple of hundred miles across the Bering Sea.

"Ah, *Libra, Libra, Libra.* You there, John?"

"Yep. Good morning, Greg."

"Ah, good morning, John. We've got you down here for Wednesday night. Is that still good?"

"Sounds good. We're still Yankee Lima on the score. And we'll need somebody to look at our deck hoist."

"Yeah, roger that. You need somebody to look at your deck hoist."

Over in the corner, Daryl Harford scribbled a note on his pad. Daryl is the shore man for the seven boats of Bill White's "Astrology Fleet": *Libra, Taurus, Aquarius, Virgo, Aries, Commodore,* and the big catcher-processor *Jeffron.*

"Ah, roger, roger, John. That's Yankee Lima, Yankee Lima." Gerhardstein looked over at an assistant, who quickly thumbed through a codebook to translate Yankee Lima to get the number of crab *Libra* had in her tanks. "Yeah, that'll be Wednesday, then, John. How's it going now?"

"Oh, getting pretty scratchy, but I figure it's the equinox. They're here somewhere."

Heads nodded in the room, as if to say, "Of course. If a Bering Sea veteran like Johnny Pirak thinks the crab are around, that's good news, good news." In the corner, though, the Beast sneered at the optimism.

"Okay, then, John. We'll see you."

"Yeah, Greg. One more thing. We'll need somebody to look at Bob's back. It's hurting him, I guess."

"Roger that, John. You need somebody to look at Bob's back. Yeah, well, good fishing. WGG65 clear."

"*Libra* clear."

"Ah, *Ocean Dynasty, Ocean Dynasty*, WGG65," Gerhardstein said then, sounding a little like Edward R. Murrow.

—⁓—

And so it went. All the scores, translated with the codebook, were grim. After a full week, the top trips would be around 90,000 pounds—250,000 would have been just okay the year before—and many, many boats were dragging in with exhausted crews and 40,000 pounds. Though the dock price paid to the fishermen at the opening was $1.27 a pound and sure to go up, most of that increase over the previous year's $.90 would be eaten up by the fuel and expenses of the longer trips and running around to find what few crab there were. In 1980, king crabbers caught more than 150 million pounds, and they thought it would last forever.

In the face of his monstrous overhead, Gerhardstein was remarkably cool. Pan Alaska had hired 400 people to run the three cooking and freezing lines at Unalaska, and the costs of food, housing, and transportation were astronomical and fixed. Down in the plant, as the first loads were coming in, the butchers, shakers, boxers, and everybody else could read the handwriting on the wall: layoffs. Even if you stayed around, it was hardly worth it to hole up in the Aleutians if, in three weeks, you work a total of forty hours. The rule for a processing worker was "No crab, no work, no money."

"The best thing about this kind of work way out here is that you can keep what you make, if you make anything," said Keith Mattson, a lead man on the case-up crew who'd been at Pan Alaska for two seasons. "Unless you're gambling or drinking it all away. The worst times are like now, when there's not a lot of work and nothing to do. Then you end up in the Elbow Room or the Unisea Inn." The "local thumping parlors," as Bering Sea raconteur George Fulton calls the Elbow Room and the Unisea, weren't quite the spectacles of years past, unless you happened to be sitting with a crew from one of the oil company exploration boats. Like a new species colonizing a remote bay, the oil folks were starting to hit Dutch Harbor, and a lot of people were waiting in line for the money Big Awl would spread around. Though the dismal crab season is totally unrelated to the oil exploration on the Bering Sea, nobody is talking about dancing with the one who brung them, so for the locals it's "Good-bye, crabbers, oh, you're a geologist, tell me all about it."

At sea, with the fleet, the rule is slightly different from the one at the packing plant: "No crab, *more work*, less money." If you're not on the crab, you have to look for them, and that means more picking and stacking of the eight-foot-square crab pots that weigh a quarter ton each, exhausted crews, more injuries, and less incentive to hit the deck alert when the skipper calls, "Showtime." And if you never find the crab—because there really aren't that many around—things get particularly grim in a way the Bering Sea fleet is not accustomed to. For quite a few years, the routine has been to run a day, spend three or four days plugging the boat, run in a day, wait in line, unload, and get out as quickly as possible. This year, the trips were seven to ten days long, unloading was a snap, and skippers and crews unconsciously found more and more reasons to stretch their time at the dock as it grew obvious that two-thirds of the crab really had disappeared.

———

"Why can't everybody just remember that this business goes in cycles," says skipper Mike Angell, laughing, on the bridge of the Bull-dog. "Some of these guys got into million-dollar boats for $10,000 down, and they're wondering why they can't keep up with the payments now. I could have done it, but I said, 'No way.' It doesn't really matter why the crab aren't here, they just aren't. It could be the water temperature. It could be overfishing. It could be that the cod and pollock ate them five years ago when they were small. Who knows?"

Others are more comfortable with someone to blame. "I'll tell you what it is," says John Pirak, master of the Libra, who had materialized out of the night with what, at that moment, was the biggest trip into Pan Alaska so far. "It's the goddamn foreign trawlers. You can't drag all over the Bering Sea and expect to have any crab left." Pirak is tired and grouchy. "You ought to make a trip with us," he says to me. "I'll show you the foreign fleet. It's like a city out there, and I'll bet half of them aren't supposed to be where they are."

Okay. A ride into the Bering Sea. "If you can't stay a full trip, we'll get you aboard a boat that's coming in. You really ought to see it out there, though," Pirak says, now on the bridge of the Libra. "And I'll show you what a season like this is all about. You have to know how to scratch; you have to pick pots until you're blind; you have to fish every area you can, too. We even went up to Norton Sound this year. And we're going to go to Adak. And then we're going to put drag gear on and learn how to trawl. You can't just give up."

Affixed to the bulkhead of Pirak's pilothouse is a plaque his crew gave him after the expedition to Norton Sound. "We are on a mission from God to pick pots for the Lord," it reads. "That's from the Blues Brothers movie," Pirak says. "You ought to see it. What it means is that this crew can pick and stack, which is all we did up there, faster than they can pick and dump. You'll see."

—⁓—

With assurances that transfer at sea in a survival suit is routine, I sail with the Libra, Pirak, and his crew. On the way out of Dutch, after dumping the dead loss crab and the garbage from the last trip, the crew assembles on deck for a beer to toast the last trip, the coming one, and the sense of teamwork that psychs these guys up for what one of them called the NFL of the fishing business. Bill, Ski, Loren, and Tom are there. A new, green teenager just joined the crew, and so far nobody has said anything at all to him. A sixth man, Bob, is in the engine room. Bob got hit by a runaway pot during tanner crab season the winter before and came away with a spinal concussion. At thirty-seven, he figures this season is the end of it for him. "I'll still fish," he says, "but not this. I'm too old, and if you can't keep up on deck, you get hurt or hurt somebody else. I've been at sea for twenty years, though, and I'm worried. I just don't do too well on land."

A day later, before we reach the grounds, Bob bends over from a wheelhouse chair to put his shoes on and can't straighten up. He will spend most of the trip in his bunk, in great pain that even the pills he has can't touch. Injuries are part of it, I'm told, and virtually every boat loses a man a year to an accident. "If you don't have injuries, you're probably not working hard enough," one man said. "Most of the time it's a bitch, though, because it's usually some guy who doesn't know what he's doing who hurts somebody who does." Everybody is leery of green men on deck, and the veterans are worried that as the paychecks get smaller, so will the skill of the crews drop off. "There will be more guys who work cheap; there will be more injuries."

Pirak decides to stop in Akutan for hanging bait and to pick up some supplies for the rest of the Astrology Fleet at the *Ultra Processor,* a crab plant on a barge that's anchored there. The crew of the *Ultra* haven't seen a crab for two days and the atmosphere aboard the big blue floater is dismal, to say the least. Tied alongside as a refrigerated warehouse and extra sleeping quarters is the *Al-Ind-Esk-a-Sea,* a navy cargo ship conversion that has taken its lumps during the past two years. "We're having a dance tonight," says an *Ultra* crew member who came to Alaska from New York City. "Maybe they'll let us have a can of beer or two. This whole thing is pretty awful. I've worked six hours since I got here, and talk about boring. There is just nothing to do, nothing but wait."

We're out of Akutan in the middle of the night and the weather changes from mild to wild. I'm accused of whistling in the wheelhouse, summoning the storm, as I sit in the galley watching *North Dallas Forty* on television. It's a movie about the National Football League, about the abuses the players suffer for the money and the fame. "The payments don't stop if the weather gets bad, so we don't stop fishing," Pirak says. "Everybody in the galley who's working to pay last year's taxes, raise your hands," another man says. Everybody laughs and pumps their arms in the air. Because the bulk of crab crewmen's income comes at the end of a calendar year, the IRS lets them defer their taxes until the following year. That worked fine until 1981.

The weather is truly frightening. In the time it takes to get to what Pirak calls his test gear, the seas build to twenty feet, the height of a two-story house, the wind to forty knots. "I sacrifice pots in places like this just in case they show up where you don't expect them to. You have to hunt them," he says. On the radar, Pirak picks up a large trawl fleet, and in an hour, we're jogging a hundred yards from a Japanese catcher boat. Its skipper smiles broadly at us from his pilothouse window as he hauls back his net. "I'll bet he's not supposed to be here," Pirak says. "He's hauling and running, you wait and see." And the skipper of that 180-foot dragger does just that, heading west to the mothership with a forty ton haul of pollock on deck.

"I call the Coast Guard all the time," Pirak says. "They get sick of hearing from me, but they never do anything about these guys. I'm a licensed master, so they have to take my protest. But they tell me the foreigners have just as much right to be here as I do, and that's bullshit. I'm going to go to London for a dragging school, and I don't want to have to compete with these guys. These are our fish."

For four days and nights, the crew of the *Libra* picks pots for the Lord, but with slim results. Pirak's coding buddies on the radio report similar low scores, and all of a sudden, even a twenty-crab-per-pot average looks like Fat City, a sickeningly low number compared with seasons past. And then it's time for me to leave, on a wild day with standing seas that make the horizon look like a saw blade in the dim light of the Bering Sea morning.

The crew streams about 150 fathoms of line astern to a Dutch-bound Astrology boat, the *Taurus*, commanded by Bob Nelsen, another veteran crabber. Then Pirak swings the *Libra* 180 degrees so we're on a closing course with the *Taurus*, 200 yards off her beam. I am on deck in a survival suit with a life ring around my middle and the line now fixed to the *Taurus* attached to the life ring. Loren gives me a shot of Wild Turkey from his going-home bottle; Bill tells me to sit on the rail, and, a few seconds later, hollers, "Jump!" I bob beside the *Libra*, frightened that I'll crash into the hull, and then I feel the tug of the *Taurus's* pot hauler and I'm on my way.

Just as I begin to relax and enjoy the ride, I pop off the crest of one of the twenty-foot swells, turn in midair, and fall back into the sea. To my horror, I am now being towed face-forward, and I realize what a sucker I am for not recognizing that dozens of things can go wrong in a deal like this. I try to shift around in the life ring, and just as I succeed at that, I look over my shoulder to see the numbers on the stern of the *Taurus*. The prop, I think. But Bob Nelsen swings the stern away from me, and moments later, pale and shaking, I am on deck and unable to stand up.

"How's fishing?" I ask, when I'm able to speak.

"Oh, not so hot," one of the crewmen says. "But they got to be here somewhere. Somebody's on 'em."

The Beast of Ugly Seasons

The crab never really came back. During the glory years from 1977 to 1981, the fleet was taking something like 150 million pounds a year; now they're lucky to get 25 million. John Pirak, like a lot of crabbers, did go trawling, the government ran the foreign fishermen off the home grounds within 200 miles of the coast, and a new boom—trawling for pollock and cod—rolled through Dutch Harbor.

Talking Price and the Cruel Sixteen

SALMON GILLNETTING * BRISTOL BAY, 1981

The 1981 Bristol Bay red salmon season proved that there is life after a market collapse. This year, the Bay delivered the pleasures of solid foreign and domestic money, a reasonably early price settlement, a healthy run of fish, and tee-shirt weather. Only a year ago, nobody seemed happy to see all the fish in the water, it rained every day, and people were walking around grouchy and somber as mourners at a funeral.

Still, your average season on the Bay is a cross between a Brazilian soccer riot and a summer camp where the counselors pass out hundred-dollar bills instead of marshmallows at the campfires. The whole show lasts just six weeks in June and July and draws an international crowd of 20,000 men and women to catch, butcher, and haul—this year—about

20 million salmon. Almost everybody starts out telling you they're up there for the money, but about ten seconds into the conversation, it's obvious that something else is going on.

The Bay itself is a gigantic funnel leading to six good-sized rivers that wash into the shallow, sandy flats of the Bering Sea. Red salmon spawn in certain kinds of river-lake-river systems, and those around Bristol Bay are perfect for them. The biggest run goes up the Kvichak River, through Iliamna Lake and into the countless tributaries and trickles around it. The other runs are smaller—on the Nushagak, Egegik, Ugashik, Togiak, and Naknek Rivers—but they, too, are legendary producers.

The village of Naknek is the home of several dozen packing plants, a pair of restaurants, and three bars. One of the restaurants, the D & D Cafe, is in an old, two-story building that was a popular spawning palace for fishermen before such activities became illegal. Right next door is Hadfield's Bar, a windowless drinking machine with a clientele that runs to locals and the older set, which on the Bay means anybody over twenty-five. The hottest song on Hadfield's jukebox this season was Bette Midler's "Stay with Me," with Blondie's "The Tide Is High" running a close second.

Just behind Hadfield's, a hundred yards away on the bluff overlooking the river, was the Naknek bureau of my magazine, the *Alaska Fisherman's Journal*. I had trouble setting it up the first night because I had forgotten to bring the stakes for anchoring the rainfly, not that I needed it. The first thing I noticed this year was that everybody was walking around with Caribbean tans waiting for the price to settle and the fish to hit. I heard right away, on June 22, that the biggest fishermen's negotiation union, the Alaska Independent Fishermen's Marketing Association (or AIFMA, which some people delighted in pointing out was an anagram for MAFIA), had just accepted an offer from Ocean Beauty Seafoods to fish for $.75 a pound, but until the other packers settled, none of the AIFMA boats would go out. When the votes were tallied, it turned out that more than 65 percent of the

AIFMA fishermen decided to accept the offer. Mitch Kink, their nego-
tiator, was going from plant to plant trying to get the other major
packers to go along with the Ocean Beauty number. I heard a little
grousing from some of the fishermen about the price because the word
filtering in from the cash buyers out in the ship anchorage was that
they were paying $.80 or even $1 already, and the price was almost
sure to go up.

When I ran into Mitch, he said he was pretty hot about the early
settlement reached across the Bay in Dillingham by the other marketing group, WACMA (Western Alaska Cooperative Marketing Association). That association's 350 members voted during the first week in
June to fish for $.65 for deliveries of salmon to be canned and $.75 for
fish to be frozen, so when Mitch went into price talks, the packers
were saying, "Gee, that WACMA number looks great to us." Later on,
Truman Emberg over at WACMA's Dillingham office told me his
members thought their price was okay and everybody just wanted to
go fishing.

A lot of people who wanted to go fishing didn't, though. The place
was loaded with drop-ins, the men and women drawn to the Bay by
the allure of money and adventure, in search of jobs. It was a cosmo-
politan group, all in all, that made the rounds of the D & D and the Red
Dog Cafe for endless cups of coffee, and the canneries and fuel docks
looking for jobs. I asked one guy from the East Coast why he came up,
and he said, "Because my mother told me not to," and went on his way.
Later I saw him on a city work crew cleaning up a minor oil spill in a
ditch by the fuel dock. I ran into Greeks, Israelis, Australians, and
Americans on the out-of-work circuit, and the bulletin boards in the
bars, post office, and canneries were jammed with their "strong and
willing to work" solicitations. One guy, wound up like a ten-cent watch
from two hours' worth of D & D coffee, said job hunting was slow
because the weather and the fishing were too good. "We need a big
storm or something," he said. "Then some of the deckhands will get
sick and tired and want to go home. Maybe in a couple of days."

As the price talks entered the final preseason hours, it became apparent that the early run predicted by Fish and Game wasn't going to materialize after all. The salmon seemed to be coming in on time for a normal peak around the first week in July, and the biologists were saying there would be about 27 million of them. Getting to Fish and Game for the daily biology line was a matter of hitchhiking from Naknek to King Salmon, about eleven miles. The road has more dips than a graph of the frozen fish market, and I came up with a bad case of frost-heave coccyx from bouncing around in the bed of a pickup that gave me a lift.

The trip was worth the bruises, though, because I ran into Chuck Meacham, Jr., the ace of the base when it comes to salmon prediction. He was sticking by his guns on the final size of the run, about 27 million, with a potential catch of 20 million to 23 million. "We thought it would be early," Meacham said, "but for some reason the fish got between Port Moller and the Naknek/Kvichak end of the Bay and they're milling around out there. It's only a matter of time, though." He told me he had gone to Japan during the winter to share prediction information with biologists there and found that both countries, for a change, agreed on the size of the run. Japanese fish brokers buy virtually all the frozen salmon from Bristol Bay, so they keep a sharp eye on the grounds.

Apparently, some of the Fish and Game salmon masters were worried about the fishing pattern that would come from good weather and a full fleet fishing from the beginning of the run instead of sitting on the beach on strike. When the efficiency of effort goes up, as it will under such conditions, the biologists start worrying about escapement, or how many fish will elude the nets to make it to the spawning beds. If the fish come all at once, or when the weather is bad, the fishing pressure isn't heavy enough to prohibit good escapement. The early word at Fish and Game was that there would be intermittent openings until the peak to guarantee the escapement, and that's what eventually happened after the price settlement. Of all the river systems, the Kvichak caused the most concern, but that's historically a later run, and eventually the escapement levels would climb to acceptable levels.

King Salmon is the airline gateway to the Bay and also the gathering point for hundreds of big-bucks foreign and American sports fishermen who come to work out on the fabulous trout and salmon rivers. Commercial fishermen hang out in King Salmon, too, when they're picking up freight or people at the airport or flying fish out on a private deal, or hitting the bars for the hell of it. And the graffiti in the men's rooms is about the best on the Bay. A sample from the bar at the King-Ko Inn: "Stick your oil money up your ass, Bristol Bay will sail again." There's a lot of sentiment against the coming offshore oil development on the Bay this year. (Big oil, for once, would actually be stopped by fishermen and the fear that the richness of the Bay would be threatened.)

In Eddie's, the other restaurant in King Salmon, I ran into a German sportsman who was completely unaware that there was a big commercial fishery cranking up on the Bay. He wondered what the action was all about and why all the people he was meeting were, as he put it, "all jazzed up." I gave him the short version of Bristol Bay madness, and he said, "Oh, I see. It's very primitive, this food gathering, you know."

The guy was short and wiry, with eyes like a starved fox, and he was dressed like an L. L. Bean ad. He told me his hobby was philosophy. How anybody can tell a total stranger that his hobby is philosophy is beyond me, and I decided to get out of there quick before the conversation got too European for me. "One minute, one minute," he said, as I started to leave. "Do you see what I mean?" I didn't want to be too rude, so I sat back down. "The whole thing is about food gathering, the way people run around, you know. It isn't just the money they come for. One of the things civilization gives us is the freedom from killing our own meat, but the killing has to be done in any case. It requires special ceremonies, special ways, and extra-ordinary places." (He said "extra ordinary" as two distinct words.) I said, "Good fishing," and headed for the road back to Naknek.

Waiting It Out with the Locals

On the way back, I decided to split the pickup torture in two and stopped between King Salmon and Naknek at Bristol Bay Contractors, an all-purpose, haul-anything, arrange-anything expediting company run by the Shawback family. The Shawbacks have been something of a one-clan population boom on the Bay for decades, and their enterprises are everywhere. They run the bus service, rent cars, sell fuel, load and unload freight, and generally service the annual onslaught of people who come for the fish. The Shawbacks also have been fishing on the Bay since the thirties and still run setnet sites and drift boats.

I found Mary Shawback, the matriarch of the family, and she told me the women and hired hands were saddling up to go put out the setnets for the next tide. Setnetters anchor their gillnets to the beach and the low-tide line and wait for the salmon to run into them at high water. They are slaves to the tides for six weeks, picking their nets on every low. "I just got a call on the radio," Mary said in her Athabascan-Irish brogue. "They settled the price." Then she started snapping orders at her beach gang while she slipped her sweatshirt over her head. "Marianne, you go get the Silver Bullet. Laverne, find out what's happening with the Ranger." She was talking about her trucks. The sweatshirt said BEACH BOSS on the back and MOMSIE on the front. "Everybody calls me Momsie, you know. But the beach boss thing, I don't know. I wish I'd had about a dozen kids; then I could be a real beach boss and not work at all," she said, laughing.

While she was talking to me, Mary was also on the radio spreading the word—or what proved to be the rumor—that the price had settled. Then we piled into the Silver Bullet, a battered gray pickup—a beach vehicle, Mary called it. The Shawbacks' setnet sites are on the beach between Naknek and Pederson Point where the sand is hard enough to drive on. Most of the sites out there are staked out by longtime residents of the area, including Alaska Governor Jay Hammond's wife, Bella. In the Silver Bullet, loaded with nets, totes, and people, and another pickup with the tracked mud-vehicle called the Ranger, the Shawback caravan started for the beach.

Flashing past the canneries along the road into town, Mary sharp-eyed the action and gradually grew concerned that no one else seemed to be getting ready to fish. "I never fish before the price is set," Mary said. "Never, never. We better stop at Whitney and ask Denton what's going on. He'll know, and besides, I have a Father's Day present for him." Father's Day had just passed, and Mary is one of the Bay's most prolific present-givers. She is also an old friend of Denton Sherry, the Whitney–Fidalgo packing company president. He heated up a lot of fishermen during the 1980 strike when he threatened to evict them from the Whitney property and generally took a hard line on the negotiations.

Everybody at Whitney was clearly anxious to go fishing, but when we found Denton, the setnet expedition had to be canceled. "No, it's not settled," said the big man with a crewcut and a neck that seemed to grow out of both shoulders. "Nobody's even come to talk to me. Not once since I met with Mitch in Seattle have I talked to him," Sherry said. "I don't know what is going on."

The season was set to open on June 23, two days away, and though some boats were scratching on the meager run starting to show up, the previous year's contracts had expired. If no settlement was reached by the 23rd, fishermen would officially be striking again. It occurred to me that Mitch Kink might be putting a championship move on Denton Sherry, the man who could have been his most immovable adversary in the price talks. I knew Mitch had been hammering at the other processing companies, I'd heard that Alaska Packers across the river in South Naknek was about ready to sign, and still nothing at Whitney, nobody talking to Denton. The strategy at that point seemed to be to ignore him and Whitney until everyone else agreed to the number.

On the Whitney dock, fishermen were rigging gear, painting their boats, and generally hanging out. The centerpiece for milling around was the gillnetter *Judy Joyce*, resting on a cradle in the middle of the dock and receiving a new coat of bottom paint. She had become the first truly independent boat on Bristol Bay way back in the fifties when Winn Brindle agreed to finance a fisherman who wanted to buy his own boat. Before that, all the boats had been owned by the canneries, and in that bit of history lay some of the background angst of AIFMA and strikes against the packing companies. Independent fishermen, of course, can't be ordered to fish.

—————

The night of June 22, the grounds were closed by Fish and Game, settlement or no settlement, to make sure enough fish were up the creek before turning the fleet loose in perfect weather. Fishing would almost certainly start the next day, so, naturally, everybody was out on the town to enjoy a last prepeak drink or stuff quarters into the battery of electronic TV games that cluttered the Fishermen's Bar at the top of the hill in Naknek. PacMan was a big hit. One guy, an accountant from a cannery, got so good at it that he could play all night for a quarter, getting free games for his scores. People stood around and cheered him.

Across the dusty Naknek main street at one point that evening, I recognized the pool-hall slouch of none other than old bored-of-fish himself, Jim Beaton, who gave me a report from the grounds. One big problem so far for the nonunion boats out there fishing had been the vast number fishing over the line. As Chuck Meacham told me, the fish were hanging out in the outer reaches of the Bay, and the temptation apparently got too great for some fishermen. Beaton was a hardworking member of the Alaska Board of Fisheries, as well as a fisherman and processing entrepreneur with his own freezer ship in the Bay. He told me stories of breakdowns and logistical nightmares that made a floating fish processor sound like a television sitcom, and went on his way.

Later, I went to the arraignments of two of the fishermen busted for fishing over the line, and I understood that there were dozens. In the cases of the two I watched, one pleaded guilty, and Judge Charles

Shawback (Mary's cousin) slapped him with a $1,500 fine with $750 suspended, a year's probation, and an order seizing three of his gill-nets and the $1,800 worth of fish found on board when he was arrested. The other fisherman, who had two recent prior convictions on similar charges, pleaded not guilty and was released on bail pending trial. His strategy was to postpone a possible conviction until the season was over because he stood to lose his limited-entry permit for a third offense.

The prosecutor, Louis Menendez, comes from a long line of fishermen and seemed to know a lot about the business. "These guys have to realize that they're not only breaking the law but threatening future generations if they don't go along with the management regulations on the fishery," he said. "We don't want to take too hard a line, but the days of the $100 fine with $50 suspended are over."

After the arraignments, the state enforcement officer invited me on a tour of the *Vigilant*, a patrol boat. I said I'd see about it, but ended up not making the trip because I got stuck during a one-day blow aboard a floating processor out in the deep-water anchorage. The fish cops had a bit of bad luck when their only helicopter piled into a river, but everybody got out okay. The over-the-line boys kept them hopping, I guess.

The night wore on and on in Naknek, the Divine Miss M sang "Stay with Me" about fifty times, Bonnie Tyler filled in from the Fishermen's Bar down the street with "It's a Heartache," and lots of fishermen got happily smashed on two-dollar beer. By noon the next day, word got around that Alaska Packers had gone for the AIFMA number, then Nelbro, then Peter Pan. Mitch said he and the members were happy with the price and ready to go fishing and that Denton Sherry had called him on the phone and said, "Bring a contract over; we're ready to go fishing." Mitch, whom one fisherman called the sleeping bear, had, it turned out, put a move on Denton, and it worked. One Whitney fisherman, though, said he would have done it differently than Mitch and taken on the toughest guy first, like in a street fight. Then, he said, everybody else would follow.

But that wasn't Mitch Kink's style, and it wasn't a year for street fighting on the Bay. The settlement was the earliest since 1975. I ran into Chuck Meacham just after the price settled when I was hanging around the Shawbacks' setnet site, and he said, "Hey, you're going to have a hard time finding something to write about this year. How do you cover happiness?"

Well, you set up your tent, and . . .

The Cruel Sixteen on an Icicle Floater

Three days after the price settlement and everybody in the Naknek fleet was singing from the same sheet of music. The salmon gazers at Fish and Game harmonized with "Don't Worry, Could Be Any Tide, Now," but their credibility sagged a bit in the face of fishing fever. After all, they were saying a week ago that the run would be five days early, and though the assembled multitudes truly believed millions of fish were on the way, an on-time peak was almost a sour note as the band tuned up for the annual rendering of "Drifting and Dreaming."

According to most of the dusty-street rumors, Egegik Bay had been the hot spot for the nonunion fishermen, a mere fifty miles southwest of the Naknek-Kvichak funnel. Many boats out there scratching were reported to be bending the Johnson Hill line to reach for the reds in that direction. The fish cops were busting a few, and fishing in a closed area was roundly condemned by the righteous lashed to their bar stools in the evenings. But the point was the fish weren't here, and they were supposed to be. Unlike the man watching his bobber and slapping his feet on river mud on a warm sunny day, the Bristol Bay drifter is not known for his patience.

Last year, the waiting days on the beach were charged off to the strike, the longest in history, but that's another matter altogether. There's no one to blame, really, no ethic to consider, and, in fact, nothing to worry about in the long run. The fish will show up. Won't they? What if they don't? What if *something* happens? What if all the sampling and predictions are just flat wrong and only 10 million come instead of 30 million? Here, let me buy this round. Bartender, get these thirsty boys a beer . . .

And then it was over. The rhythms on the morning of the fourth day of waiting changed from adagio to allegro, and Blonde Kate at the D & D Cafe leaned with her elbows on the counter, there in her do-rag to keep the curl in her hair, worrying that the Greek would get grouchy when his business fell off and wondering how she'd get the money for her "operation" back in Memphis. She'd been telling me about it for days. That morning, I was alone at nine o'clock on the eating side of the cigarette-pocked Formica, and I muttered, for the first time, advice to her: "Go down to the fuel dock and try to get on a boat."

In repose, the Naknek fuel dock is an ordinary fixture no different from those in dozens of Alaskan ports, but with the biggest salmon run in the world on tap, it was a scene from a James Cagney riot movie. Several hundred boats were jammed together in the shallows, their skippers jockeying for one of about thirty spots at the pier. The boats came alongside and side-tied in bobbing rows out from the face of the dock timbers, sometimes finding space smoothly in turn, sometimes careening like drunks in the parking lot of a country and western bar. The bounders were jeered and cursed when they butted in line, but were never forced out because that would slow things down—and speed is essential. Everyone wanted to get out of the river before the next falling tide slammed the door.

So I was at the fuel dock waiting for the human interest story that would materialize if Blonde Kate threw her apron on the floor and came down to hit up one of these cowboys for a job, and I ran into no less than the chairman of the board of Icicle Seafoods, Bob Thorstensen, who was leaning on a piling cap surveying the scene. I didn't recognize him right off; he had the shades and baseball hat on, naturally, and the salt-and-pepper halibut jacket, but he seemed more like a kind-of-old guy looking for a chance than one of the founders of the biggest fish company in Alaska.

One of his tenders, the *Chichagof*, was flush to the pier just under where the chairman was standing, and I finally put it together. "Hi, Bob." "Howdy, Brad." And we're off and running. Five minutes later, I was introduced to the *Chichagof's* skipper, Joe Carlo, who said his breakfast cruise out to the ship anchorage was leaving within the hour, and if I could get my gear together in time, I was welcome. The chairman invited me to spend time on one of his floating processors, the *Bering Star*, and I said deal me in and took off to find my kit and Movie Bidness. (Blonde Kate never showed up.)

I finally found Movie Bidness in the house-called-home-by-many, and he was in a foul mood when I woke him. Bidness had one of the greatest hustles I've ever seen, on the Bay or anyplace else, with his green, waterproof box full of movie cameras, a D. W. Griffith hat he wore turned around backward, and the perfect answer when somebody asked him what the hell he was doing. "I'm making a movie," he'd say. "What about?" the other guy'd say. And people, especially women, would show him their best tricks while Bidness pointed one of his cameras at them. I never did know if he even had film in the damn things, except that every so often he'd crouch down somewhere with both hands in a black bag. "Changing film," he'd say. But you never knew.

Which is routine on the Bay. Movie Bidness and I were like endangered species during the 1981 season. The year before, anybody who could walk, crawl, and hold a pencil or a camera was up to cover the big strike; not so this year. When I ran into Bidness the day I got into King Salmon, we agreed to swap exotic transportation arrangements, and the chairman's offer of a few days on a floater qualified.

The chairman had disappeared by the time we made it back to the fuel dock, and so had the *Chichagof*, but we saw the tender at anchor out in the river and hitched a ride out on a fish boat. Bidness did his thing with the camera, and I talked to a teenage deckhand from Pittsburg, California, who figured 100,000 pounds of Bristol Bay red salmon a year equaled a used Pontiac Trans Am with a trunk full of drugs and nothing but steelhead fishing, duck hunting, and Malibu Barbies for the rest of his life. His eyes glowed when I told him I heard cash buyers out in the ship anchorage were already paying $1 a pound. Step right up.

Aboard the *Chichagof*, it turned out that the chairman wasn't kidding about a breakfast cruise; we ate on the five-mile run out to the river mouth, soaking up that special fish-tender hospitality. Skipper Joe Carlo, like all good tendermen, is a blend of mariner, stevedore, and country club bartender, with the easy pace that is always a welcome counterpoint to the mad rush of actual fishing. Stopping for a breath aboard a packer is an old tradition, and it takes a certain kind of personality to buy fish on the grounds.

During the season, the ship anchorage at a point called the "Y" between the Naknek and Kvichak Rivers is probably the fifth-largest city in Alaska. A hundred ships, tenders, processors, freighters, and barges are anchored out there from the middle of June to the end of July like a portable archipelago. A slight chop was running as the *Chichagof* wove through the ships, heading for the *Bering Star*. Bidness ran all over the place, whirring away at the passing splashes of color and seagoing shapes: the big *Pacific Pride*, looking like a queen's yacht with her railed shelter deck and bright, white paint job; the *Lady Pacific*, looking like a cross between a barge and a crabber with her Bristol Bay outboard—a Japanese tramper—alongside. The big crab boats were there in force, picking up the off-season packing nickel: the *Aleutian Mistress*, *Taurus*, *Norseman*, *Big Blue*, *Northern Leander*, *Moriah*, and dozens of others. Like attending drones, skiffs were buzzing among ships and boats in the anchorage, and even the air was alive with choppers and light planes flying right down on the decks under the low-lying scud.

Then we saw the *Star*, with her freighters moored to her port side and the tug, née oil-field supply boat, *Trans Pac* to starboard. As we hove to, the entire assemblage looked as if it were ignoring the sea altogether, sitting rock solid with the big, blue shape of the processing barge towering in the center. The *Chichagof* was bouncing on the morning lump, and Movie Bidness pointed out that our chances of getting off without either falling into the Bay or taking a soaking from the spray were slim. Both of us began preparing ourselves for what was sure to be a very bad moment.

But we made it unscathed and were standing on the sponson of the barge for handshakes before I had a chance to back out of the deal. First, there was Kim Suelzle, who introduced himself as the manager. Then a stunning woman who dashed up to me and Bidness and said, "Welcome to the *Boring Star*," and disappeared through a hatch in the wall and into the maw of what looked like a fifty-foot-high chrome-blue warehouse before Bidness even got his camera out. Then we met Tim Garborino, who said he was the assistant manager.

The *Bering Star* is a converted military oceangoing barge, once named the *Thunderbird*. She was reportedly used to haul frozen food to the Philippines and to haul bananas or something like that back to the States. The barge is 255 feet long, 55 feet wide, and draws 10 feet, carries a processing crew of 120 during salmon season, and can crank out 230,000 pounds of headed, gutted, frozen reds a day, or 300,000 pounds frozen whole. Icicle Seafoods bought her from the government in the fall of 1978, hired its own crew for the conversion, and by the spring of 1979, the *Bering Star* was on the grounds going head to head with a similar-looking processor, the *Ultra Processor*. The *Ultra* ran into a bit of bad luck when it dragged anchor and grounded, but so far, no such evil fate had befallen either the *Bering Star* or the other Icicle processor, the *Arctic Star*.

"Every link of the anchor chain weighs 85 pounds," Suelzle said while were were up in the office (there's no bridge or wheelhouse on a barge). "The anchor itself weighs 20,000 pounds, and we can't even pick it up ourselves. When we move, the *Trans Pac* has to come around front and pick up the anchor with her crane. Make yourselves at home."

Home for 120 very alert, stainless-steel kids—only a half-dozen souls on board were older than thirty—is spread over three decks, four if you count the living vans lashed to the top of the barge. Our tour was a parade led by Suelzle but joined en route by others drawn by the curiosity of new blood aboard. We began in the freezers, the lowest deck. There, overseen by freezer rats, the fish are blast-frozen and sometimes stored if a tramper is not tied alongside to receive the salmon. Usually, though, the freezers are just part of a processing line that begins with a gillnet and moves with little interruption until boxes of frozen salmon are tucked into the hold of a Japanese freighter.

Above the freezers is the processing deck, home of the "cruel sixteen," as Suelzle calls the long shifts the crew works when the peak of the run hits. The processing, egg house, freezer, and case-up crews work in three overlapping sixteen-hour shifts. If, at the end of a shift, you're not hallucinating, it probably means you'd been dogging it or that you were crazy to start with. When we walked through the processing deck on that first day, the place had a weird stillness to it. The lights were on. The knives were sharp. The four stainless-steel butchering tables gleamed. It was like a major-league locker room before a playoff game, a place with a clear and singular purpose.

"The waiting is driving everybody nuts," said one of the marchers, a woman of about twenty who looked like a debutante slumming in oilskins. "No fish, no money, no rhythm. That's the way it goes. In two weeks, we'll be tired and sore and sorry we're here, but that's much better than this, because everybody knows why we're here. Money and Zen." Bidness shot me a look that said, "Anybody who is saying stuff like 'money and Zen' on the processing deck of this slab has to be in the movie," so he started unpacking the cameras and answering the usual questions.

We all headed to the galley which adjoins the processing room in the bow of the barge, for the first of about a hundred cups of *Bering Star* coffee that I would drink during the next three days. The galley is set up like a dollhouse cafeteria and seats fifty shoulder to shoulder. On the wall is a chalkboard for keeping track of the crew bonus, paid at the end of the season as a production incentive. The galley is one of only two common spaces on the barge—the other is a TV room on the living deck—and the social center for the crew. Time disappears very quickly on the *Star,* as it does in a Vegas casino, where purpose far overshadows chronology; it is always simultaneously midday, morning, and midnight in the galley.

At the tables are the talkers, backgammon players, loners, letter-writers, eaters, and Risk junkies, who play the board game of global war nonstop over by the coffee urn. The food, served in full meals four times a day with light meals in between, is excellent. Everything in the galley seems like a miniature except the people, who, forced by circumstances, work their minds around to a very pragmatic and unique illusion of privacy in always-cramped quarters.

The living deck, reached by steep ladders from the processing room, is laid out around a narrow, rectangular passageway with inside and outside rooms, each for four or six people. The men's and women's showers are connected by a big sauna, the most extravagant use of space on the *Star.* Also on the living deck are the office and radio room, and the TV room, where closed-circuit movies and prime-time programming run twenty-four hours a day. The hot favorites during my time on the *Star* were *Star Trek: The Movie* and *One Flew Over the Cuckoo's Nest.* During the former, the audience, on beanbag pillows, played off the lines of Captain Kirk, Spock, and Scotty like comedians; during the latter, everybody had a good cry. "The *Star,* after all, is a cross between a spaceship and an insane asylum," said the debutante.

Just moving through the narrow passageway required lessons. I took one from Lawrence, easily the oldest citizen aboard, who appeared phantasmagorically with a broom in his hand. He blended into the wall to let me pass. Five paces down the two-and-a-half-foot-wide aisle, I realized I was going in the wrong direction and turned to pass Lawrence, this time going in the opposite direction. Again he hit the wall and froze. At that point, a woman in a tank top walked right at me, so I hit the wall next to Lawrence, and he looked down at me— he's a tall man—but quickly averted his eyes. Instinctively, I headed back in my original direction, figuring I'd rather follow that woman than wander lost and alone in the passageway, and Lawrence, without any other acknowledgment of my third passing, hit the wall. After that, I wanted to talk to Lawrence more than anyone else on the barge, but he looked away every time I said anything to him. A quiet man.

Above the living deck, on what amounts to the roof of the barge, are ten-by-twenty-foot shipping vans converted to house ten people each, stacked like cordwood when they sleep. On top of two of them is the chopper pad, where Icicle's own Valkyrie touches down to deliver mail, supplies, and people. Movie Bidness decided that the chopper would make a hot shot, and from then on he was always listening for the turbine whine, never missing a landing or take-off. Aft from the living vans are enormous piles of cardboard for fish cases, covered with tarps of bright blue and red that give the deck a kind of camping trip atmosphere and provide many nooks and crannies for solitude in the open air. The view of the anchorage from the top of the *Star* was spectacular, and during the leisure hours before the salmon showed up, it was the Riviera for sunbathers. When the barge's water-makers are not on the blink, the top deck also sports a genuine hot tub.

Movie Bidness started getting itchy after we finished the tour, settled into our cramped staterooms, and generally accepted our roles on the barge as creatures from another planet. He figured he wanted to film the progress of a fish from tender to freezer, and then get off the barge and try to find a fishing skipper who would let him get that part of the chain. On the barge, the waiting continued, though, since processors are about a day behind fishermen when waiting for the fish to show up.

We killed time in the galley, and went to a crew meeting where Suelzle passed out fifty-dollar bills to the winners of the backgammon tournament and a hundred dollars to the winner of the weekly safety drawing. Anyone who has not been hurt during the previous week is eligible to win the hundred dollars. Suelzle, talking more like a therapist than a processing plant superintendent, also told the crew about arrangements for R & R in Anchorage when the *Star* was being towed to Prince William Sound for the late-summer season. He told jokes, stroked some of the crew members, and asked for suggestions. Then he delivered the real news, giving the evening line on the arrival of the run. "Get some sleep. The tenders will start coming in late tonight with fish," he said. And the atmosphere in the galley changed instantly. Bidness took everybody's picture through his wide-angle lens, and caught up in the work-hungry mood, I asked Suelzle if I could work a shift on the sliming line.

The next morning, after a night of saunas, brandy, two cans of blast-freezer-chilled beer, and no sleep, I am standing at a butcher table in clean, yellow oilskins. Much to the amusement of the others at my table, I am trying to learn the knife strokes that will allow me to gut about ten fish a minute without hurting myself.

Only 30,000 fish have been delivered—a mere three-hour tune-up for the real thing when the cruel sixteens start—but for me the short shift seems like a lifetime. I spend the first hour learning the routine and generally holding up the line, and when I finally get it down, I find out what the debutante was talking about when she babbled about Zen. Once you know how to do it, there is no room for structured thought on the sliming line. Music blares from speakers mounted over the lines, the fish never stop coming, your arms and legs get numb, and your mind wanders. It is actually peaceful, amidst all the gore of the line. Quickly, my yellow slicker is covered with flecks of blood and tissue, and there is no way to connect real life to my spot at the table. Around me, people's expressions are sublime smiles; grins and frowns seem to come from nowhere. Some sing their own songs over the howling speakers; some chatter intermittently over the din of the machines, often to themselves. The single connection among the slimers is the fish, and the occasional playful flick of a salmon heart across the table to smack someone's neck or forehead. At one point, I catch a heart in my eye, which cripples everyone with laughter. I am blinded, and the woman next to me tenderly offers me a clean spot on the back of her shoulder for me to wipe out the blood. I learn the heart flip during the next hour. Movie Bidness takes everybody's picture and says he'll work the line from now on.

Time flew on the line, plodding only when, for one reason or another, the fish were held up in the bins. And then it was over.

The next day was the same, but longer, as the hours on the line increased with the run. At the numb-arms-and-legs stage, Bidness and I agreed that we had to get off the *Star* at any cost and really soon. After the shift, we asked Suelzle to order up the chopper for the first thing the next morning and proceeded with the sauna, brandy, and beer routine again. The blow started at about midnight, and by nine the next morning it was a full gale. The trampers let go from the port side of the barge to anchor in uncluttered water nearby, as did the *Trans Pac* from the starboard, and the *Bering Star* began a waltz-time wallow that had many in the crew talking to God on the big white phone. "A lot of these people are scared to death of the sea," Suelzle said. "Some weren't even aware that a processing plant could be a floater until they got here. And, oh yeah, the chopper is out of the question until this thing flattens out."

Bad news. Movie Bidness and I were about to learn about barge fever, since we were, to put it mildly, very ready to get off, had said our good-byes, and didn't even have the prospect of the slime line to take our minds off the feeling that we were trapped. The gale, of course, prohibited the transfer of fish from the tenders, and, well, that's life.

The wind finally eased up in the late afternoon, and at dinner we got word that the chopper was coming to deliver an inspector from Lloyd's of London, insurers of the barge, who wanted to inspect the anchorage. We were assured that the Lloyd's man was making a routine visit, but there was little doubt that the *Ultra Processor's* misfortune had the insurance company on its toes when it came to processing barges.

On the pad, with the wind still kicking up to twenty knots or so, the pilot wound the engine way up before popping the chopper loose, so we sprung violently away from the *Star*. Jammed into the back seat with our gear, Movie Bidness and I slipped on the intercom head-phones that were hanging in front of us, and I heard the pilot whistling "Ride of the Valkyries," off-key but loudly, as the chopper turned west into the sun, roaring over the tundra toward Dillingham.

—⁓—

The big floating-freezer barges spelled the end of the century-long hegemony of the on-shore canneries. Since the barges brought their own fishermen with them, the unions that were once tightly bound to the canneries also softened their grip on the Bay. Eventually, Japanese buyers would completely control red salmon from Bristol Bay and buy most of the production capacity in Alaska. In 1996, fishermen filed a class-action suit claiming price fixing in a cornered market.

The Billion-dollar Bottomfish Dream

GROUNDFISH TRAWLING · KODIAK, 1985

As we sink through the clouds on approach to the Kodiak airport, I remember that the runway ends at the foot of a mountain and is routinely lashed by icy squalls and crosswinds. Swell. I slam back the last of my drink and mutter a winter-flying-in-Alaska mantra, the gist of which is: I'll take any landing I can walk away from. We break clear of the overcast, with the 737 twin-jet jinking and shuddering while, a couple of hundred feet below, the black surface of the sea is shredded into bright streaks by the frightening wind that has even stripped the pretense of ease from the flight attendants lurching along the aisle checking seat belts.

A missed approach at Kodiak is like missing the deck of an aircraft carrier, and I hear the engines spool up to full power for a go-around if the landing goes bad. Now we're less than a hundred feet over the sea, and for just a moment the landing lights of the bucking jet reveal a trawler just below us, her working deck taking green water. I see a figure just aft of the wheelhouse, though, apparently not in distress and waving. Why, I think, am I not drawn to writing about warm, calm places instead of the fishing grounds of the North Pacific Ocean? Then the plane shudders and drops as if it's been smacked by an invisible hand, and for a bad moment I know I'm not the only one on that sucker who thinks it might actually come apart in the air. Out the window, the wing on my side is flapping like it's made of paper, and I feel the blood drain from my face. The guy next to me, who hasn't uttered a word except "Two V.O. and Sevens" since we left Anchorage, says to me, "Take it easy. Kodiak isn't the end of the world; you can only see it from here."

Now, on reflection, I figure that was a rude comment about a picturesque fishing town that, for five years, had been churning out money faster than a gang of counterfeiters in a suburban garage. Ever since the fleets perfected techniques for turning king crab into Porsches, big steel boats, and gold neck chains, Kodiak had ranked number one or two in the value of seafood landed in U.S. ports. I flew into Kodiak on that snotty March day in 1981 because we also had learned to turn king crab into newspapers through the magic of advertising. There were five full-blown monthlies covering the fisheries off Alaska and the West Coast, all feeding off a frenzy of electronics manufacturers, shipyards, and chandlers of every sort doing business in the boom. I was a writer for one of them, and my paper was featuring Kodiak—Alaska's quintessential port—in the May issue. I needed lots of photographs, local color, and a close-up piece on what was being billed as the "Billion-dollar Bottomfish Dream."

The Plot

In the Dream, which had two competing variations, American fishermen took over the offshore grounds and the 2 million metric tons of

cod, pollock, sole, and rockfish that hungry foreign fleets were currently catching within 200 miles of our coast. The Dream made hot
copy, since the king crab boom showed every indication that it would
bust soon. Everybody wanted to believe that some stable, year-round
fishery could take its place. It would also shore up the flaky salmon
business that went from good years to bad years like the stock market.

So the day after cheating death in the sky, there I was aboard the
new $4.5 million, 123-foot Marco-built trawler *Storm Petrel*, getting set
to cheat death in the Gulf of Alaska. A chance encounter at the airport
had led me to the skipper, George Fulton, an old friend who offered to
take me with him on a cod prospecting trip. We sailed from the weath-
ered dock of the Alaska Food Company, an old plant once run by the
New England Fish Company, a venerable, family-owned institution
that didn't survive the shift to corporate hardball during the runaway
inflation of the later seventies. With the help of healthy state and federal subsidies, the Kodiak plant had been converted to process bottomfish as part of the Alaskan version of the Dream.

The Alaskan quest for the Dream began in 1979 when the governor hired some big-time consultants to tell the state just what it wanted
to hear: that the bottomfish—cod, pollock, rockfish, and flatfish—off
Alaska's coast could drive a stable, billion-dollar industry in just twenty
years. The trick would be to make sure the fish were processed in
plants on shore, in Alaskan towns, by Alaskan workers, and taxed by
the state for the good of all.

Naturally, the very next year, the state of Washington hired big-
time consultants to tell its fishermen what they wanted to hear about
the Dream—that America can best develop its fisheries in the 200-
mile zone off Alaska with a fleet of high-volume, Washington- and
Oregon-based catcher boats, factory trawlers, and motherships using
technology and methods similar to those of the foreign fleets that
would soon be run out of the zone. Joint ventures with the foreigners
would be ideal, the consultants said, for easing into the action, gaining
access to markets, and learning how to fish in large-scale operations.

The emotional voltage surging between the Alaskans and the "Forces of the South" (as one politician put it) can be traced to sources that turn well-mannered people into junkyard dogs at worst and treacherous adversaries at best. Alaskans have been gagging for a couple of hundred years on an economic motif best described as "take the money and run." For a hundred of those years, for instance, the canned salmon industry had been run as a cash cow by a handful of Seattle families. Way back, there had been the Russians and the fur trade and renegade masses with gold fever. Most recently, it had been Texans and oil, and the Alaskans didn't want a blooming U.S. offshore industrial fleet cashing in on the Bottomfish Dream and just hitting ports up north every once in a while to bust up the bars and buy groceries.

As for the Forces of the South, they were staring down the business end of market-rate loans and runaway inflation. Such conditions put them in the mood to fight fiercely for a more stable future on the bottomfish grounds. They were also of a mind to let the Alaskans know they don't own the North Pacific Ocean. And even as I lay aboard the *Storm Petrel* outbound in a blow with the weather boards up in my berth, the Forces of the South had mustered in a joint venture nearby. About eight American trawlers were just across Kodiak Island in Shelikof Strait, slugging the huge spring pollock school and delivering to Korean factory ships at sea. It was perfect practice for a fledgling distant-water fleet. Meanwhile, the *Storm Petrel* was off to demonstrate the feasibility of delivering reasonably fresh, bled Pacific cod to a shore plant.

I had never been on a trawler before, but I was sailing with a fisherman made-to-order for the Alaskan Dream. Or so I thought. George Fulton is an articulate, sardonic man in his early fifties who has fished all his life, mostly out of foreign ports whose names I cannot pronounce, and who wrote a book about his adventures. After reading *Good Morning, Captain*, I realized that Fulton had come to his cynicism and independence quite naturally by just taking a good look at the world and its inhabitants, most of whom don't have enough to eat. He once ran a fleet of fishing boats for an African nation where good fishing meant the locals wouldn't have to eat roots and dirt for a few days. If a guy knew how to fish, he was a very important person. Fulton also has been part-owner of a brothel in South America, has fled a couple of coups, and is married to an international ice-skating coach who tolerates his endless sea time.

When I first met him, Fulton had been fishing the Alaskan grounds long enough to have earned a reputation as an occasionally charming raconteur and something of a hard-ass—a character. Some people said he was a screamer on a boat, but his deck boss had fished with him for more than a decade, and many of the crewmen who had passed through his fo'c'sles said he was worth the time. One guy told me George lived his life as if it were some kind of private joke or a concoction he'd just thought up. His presence dominated, whether by raised voice or the quiet dignity of this graying, glaring, bulky fisherman who could have doubled for Wolf Larson in a bad mood. And George knew himself pretty well, too. On his bridge, a prankster had screwed on a brass plaque that read: "If you can't dazzle them with brilliance, baffle them with bullshit." George let it stay.

We were running for the Semidi Islands to the west, in the bight where the Aleutian Chain transforms itself into mainland Alaska. I was vilely seasick for a day and a night, but by the second morning in mercifully calm seas, I was on the job. I left my berth for the galley, where the hours were filled with small chores, card playing, and lots of coffee. The galley was fitted with stereo equipment, a television set and tape player, and all the conveniences of a professional kitchen, and was decorated with a few of Muriel Fulton's paintings, hung above an off-yellow, Naugahyde-cushioned couch. The cabin smelled of diesel fuel, new linoleum, and damp clothes.

The pleasantries required of a stranger in as intimate a setting as a fishing boat took several hours. I met the crew, whom George called the Stainless-steel Kids, three of them under the direction of a man who clearly was no kid, the deck boss John. One of the kids told me he was twenty-three and had been at sea since he was sixteen. Without a note of self-aggrandizement or romanticism, he also told me he had no home other than his berth, and that he was sailing with Fulton to learn trawling, a collection of skills he figured would be his meal ticket for as long as he needed one. He and the others—a greenhorn deckhand and a woman who was studying for her mate's papers—talked about net mending, electronics, and refrigeration systems with the same enthusiasm most kids their ages reserve for cars, ski gear, and rock-and-roll. George watched me watching them; I suppose the kids put on the dog a bit for the visitor.

The Dream Goes Bust

When George Fulton and I turned our attention to each other, I laid my thoughts about the Billion-dollar Bottomfish Dream on him. I wanted his opinions on who he thought would be the winners and losers and why. His reaction to my spiel on the Alaskans and the Forces of the South came wrapped in gestures of impatient amusement. He exhaled cigarette smoke, glared down at the Formica table top, looked away from me, and spit a fragment of tobacco from the end of his tongue to the deck. Then he turned to me with his head cocked and his face wrinkled in thought and laughed right in my face. He said something like "You really believe all that crap is important, don't you?" And I'm thinking, brother, I'm looking at five more days with the guy and already I'm a target.

Then he softened and told me a story about the time Muhammad Ali, the great boxer, bought 50,000 tons of whole, frozen pollock on the spur of an inspired moment from a fish broker he was having dinner with in Caracas, Venezuela. Ali shipped the pollock to a cold storage in New York City with plans to sell it at cost in predominantly black neighborhoods to introduce cheap protein for the masses. But Ali, the old floating butterfly, hadn't counted on the fact that, right then, New York City blacks wouldn't buy, cook, and eat a pollock unless they were literally starving. Supposedly, the fish he bought is still sitting there in a freezer.

Fulton asked me if I got the point. I shook my head. Then he laughed at me again, a guttural smoker's cackle. He said he thought people would eventually get hungry enough to eat just about anything that swims or crawls and that all the political bickering, chauvinism, and such were just background noise to the powerful music of a hungry world with an exploding human population. "Who cares who catches it?" he asked me. "I'll work for anybody—Americans, Koreans, Japanese, whatever." The big picture, he said, is all that matters.

On that trip on the *Storm Petrel* I eventually abandoned my search for the Dream in favor of the clearer sensibilities of the sea. I left behind the details, images, and manipulations that seduce politicians and journalists and found the source of a fascination that carried me through hundreds of fish-press deadlines over the next three years.

On the pitching deck of the Storm Petrel, with the shudder of the trawl shaking us from the deep, I came to understand that money has very little real meaning in the scheme of things to do with fishing. In a collection of images and events that remain crystalline even three years after they loped through my mind, I saw fishermen and fishing—in fact, all human activity—stripped to queer and frightening primitive terms. There was the Big Picture, hung in a glowing frame against the background of the dark, wild ocean near the Semidi Islands.

In the Lunch Line

We were trawling to compile what George called a "cod history." Along the hundred-fathom edge just north of the Aleutian Trench, he hoped to find what few Pacific cod had not made their way into the depths for the summer. Even if he caught nothing, he'd know more about when the spawning rush begins for that area if the cod were already gone. The great upwelling from the 4,000-fathom trench is

one of nature's mightiest lunch lines, constantly replenishing the zooplankton and invertebrates that anchor the food web. The currents
carry the food up onto the great flats of the continental shelf that links
Asia and North America beneath the Bering Sea. In the Arctic, the
shelf grows even broader in its westward transformation into the Sibe-
rian and Chukchi Seas, which lie north of the Russian taiga. Vaster
than the rich banks of the North Atlantic, the Arctic flats are perfect
for trawling because of the shallow water, relatively even subsea terrain, and, above all, the presence of an edible mass of crab, fish, and
the things they eat unsurpassed anywhere on Earth.

By the mid-1970s, foreign fleets were taking about 1.1 million metric tons of bottomfish within 200 miles of the Alaskan coast and another
4 million metric tons elsewhere in the North Pacific and Bering Sea.
The total of 5.1 million metric tons equals 11.2 billion pounds of edible
protein. By comparison, all U.S. and Canadian fishermen from California to the Bering Sea take only a million metric tons annually of all
other species combined, including bottomfish, crab, and salmon.

Most of our hauls that trip on the *Storm Petrel* were pollock, though
there were enough cod mixed in to send the crew on deck to cull them
out, bleed them by slitting their throats just behind the gills, and pitch
them into chilled brine in the tanks. The pollock and everything else
that came up in the trawl was dumped back into the sea through the
scuppers. I was told to stay out of the way until I got the feel of the
deck and the rhythm of the work. So I went to the bridge and watched
George move expertly among the arrays of sophisticated electronic
fishing gear as naturally as most of us move around a car radio. In a single day, he could plot and record more about the submarine terrain
and presence of distinct species of fish than a skipper just ten years ago
could have come up with in an entire season. Fulton told me the plotter was the most revolutionary piece of gear handed to fishermen since
depth sounding came along after World War II. He told me he was a
little worried that such powerful tools could allow us to overfish and
kill off the resource's ability to recover.

On the working deck, the main trawling wires led off the stern from a pair of winches, each the size of a Honda Civic. The wires vibrated as if they were massive jumper cables running off the boat into the sea, down to the heart of the Dream. In the water astern, the net surfaced during each haulback, sometimes bloated with the pressure-inflated bodies of the fish, sometimes empty, sometimes snarled by a lost crab pot. Over the floating net, the sun would flash off the gulls.

After a day of watching, tending the coffee, and racking up an embarrassing string of cribbage victories, like Tom Sawyer I was suckered and allowed to cut cod on deck. With a knife I sharpened razor fine on a big stone in the galley, I slit hundreds of Pacific cod just behind the gills and picked up a backache I will never forget. Many hauls brought odd creatures, rare fishes, each one delighting the working crew. They poked through the flopping, quivering mass of flesh that spilled from the net looking for cod, of course, but pleased when the oddities turned up. The work made them happy, despite the black seas rising above the rails and the frightening trawl cables a heartbeat away.

By the fourth day of the trip, I was a fairly regular member of the cod-cutting crew, out there on every haul slashing away with the long knife. Late in the afternoon, just as the swells were taking on that extra shade of black that precedes darkness, I felt the *Storm Petrel* shudder on a slightly different frequency than the one that usually went with her corkscrew roll. The deck plating shivered for a moment with the vibrations of powerful machinery, and overhead the cable whined a different chord. I looked up, startled, toward the bridge, hoping, I suppose, for some reassuring sign from George. As I did, he stormed out of the wheelhouse onto the wing of the bridge, shaking his head and roaring over the roar of the winches and the sea. The cables made even more tortured sounds and then settled into a steady howl. The net, when it finally surfaced, was in tatters.

We had apparently snagged on a rock pile or some other unseen objection to our trawl. Since the day was nearly done, trawling ceased and the mending began. I watched from the bridge wing, unable to help, while George and John taught the green crew how to fix the trawl, a chore that went on late into the night. Wielding needles of twine, their hands flew.

The weather worsened. Rain began to fall, its fresh drops often inseparable from the spray blowing from the sea. The working deck was lit by bright halogen lights, but a foot beyond the rail was a black curtain, bringing the same fears that come when you cannot see beyond the light of a campfire in the wilderness. George and his crew talked a kind of grumbling jive while they worked, never rushing, either maintaining good cheer or simply keeping silent if necessary when the cold and fatigue pressed down on them. My mind roamed.

The Big Picture

According to reputable futurists, many, many people who are alive today will be competing fiercely for food before they die. The point here is far more basic than whether the economic winner of the contest to live the Bottomfish Dream will be the Alaskans or the Forces of the South. Food has become such a certainty in most of the United States that we have lost track of how special our situation is in a global context. For most of the 35,000 years or so our species has been around, we have not had enough to eat at least as often as those times when food was abundant. Hunger has been a familiar, dark companion. The big steam in the boiler of the Bottomfish Dream is fired by our bare-fanged instinct to control food.

When the story of my trip with George Fulton and the *Storm Petrel* ran in the magazine, the headline was "Alaska Food Company Brings Bottomfish Dream 110 Tons Closer to Reality." It was matter-of-fact reporting that reflected little of what I've related here. A month and a half later, Alaska Food went belly up in the ditch when politics favored the withdrawal of loans and subsidies. At the time, only one other shore plant was buying cod and that was out in Dutch

Harbor, where Norwegians had fronted the money for a salt-packing operation. A couple of other outfits, including the Reverend Sun Myung Moon's Universal Seafoods in Kodiak, were running test batches of cod and pollock.

When the crab fishery went down the next year, it did not do so gradually; it collapsed like a dynamited building. By the winter of 1983, the new, beautiful, steel crabbers were parked on repo row in Seattle's Fishermen's Terminal with pathetic Christmas lights in their rigging. That winter, the line getting the most laughs was "If you sign up for a new checking account at a Seattle bank, you get your choice of a free gift—a toaster or a crab boat."

The smart money went elsewhere, of course, into joint ventures. A couple of big factory ships are in the works on the West Coast in 1985, and one syndicate tried running a leased German factory ship in an all-U.S. venture, but it failed. In Alaska, the Bottomfish Dream is soft-pedaled now. There's a new administration, and the budget for the Bottomfish Development Office dropped from $7 million to about $500,000. George Fulton is working the *Storm Petrel* 320 days a year in joint ventures and packing a little salmon in the summer. He calls the salmon packing "yachting with a $4.5 million boat."

And these days, I'm watching the Dream unfold in the chiller case at the supermarket down the street.

———

Alaska's Bottomfish Dream came true, and seventeen years
after the Storm Petrel *delivered those few loads to*
Kodiak, on-shore and offshore fleets are going great guns.
The pollock, cod, and flatfish are allocated specifically to
each fleet, to avoid the conflicts that were part of every-
body's worst-case scenario. And in 1996, the Alaskans
went a step further and seized control of 15 percent of the
total Gulf of Alaska quota for Pacific cod, to be fished
exclusively within state waters out to three miles. The
U.S.-flag factory trawlers have been so successful in

American waters that many are also fishing off South
America and around the world, dominating the global
fisheries scene.

Kenny and the Council

Fishermen never seem comfortable in windowless rooms. Most of the time they fidget.

Arni Thomson, an offshore crabber, is tapping on the white linen covered table with a pen; Barry Fisher, a trawler, is talking at the moment and tracing unfathomable shapes in the hazy air with his cigarette; Larry Cotter, a labor organizer who isn't a fisherman but might as well be, appears motionless until you notice the minute adjustments he constantly makes to the position of his eyeglasses on the table next to his chairman's gavel. Pete Islieb, a salmon hand, is settled in his chair in a hunch, nodding at what Fisher is saying, something distinctly conciliatory about crabbers and trawlers in the Bering Sea.

Then a biologist is talking. Otto is his name, and among these fishermen, something in his bearing gives him away as a member of a different tribe. He is detached and aloof, not unpleasantly to be sure, but somehow apart from the others, who, quite simply, are people who operate closer to the edge than he does. Thompson interrupts the biologist, then Fisher interrupts Thompson, then somebody laughs, and then comes the sound of Cotter's gavel. In the small room, it's like the noise a baseball bat makes launching a hard line drive. In the instant of silence that follows, the tobacco odors and the flat smell of the filtered hotel air compete for the senses.

"One at a time, please," Cotter says. But even he succumbs, like the others have, to the temptation to add an aside about the tedious divergence on so simple a matter as Otto's statistics that has infected the discussion. "It's no wonder decisions like this one are made by politics. It's almost impossible to come up with a biological solution," he says, clipping the ends of his words in a way that is familiar to anybody who has watched Cotter navigate through the political waters of the North Pacific for the past decade.

These people belong to a work group of the Advisory Panel—the AP, as it's called—to the North Pacific Fishery Management Council. The council is also meeting, in the ballroom across the lobby from the AP. The full Advisory Panel has twenty-five members who officially represent the collective wishes and wisdom of the fishing fleet, their political organizations, seafood processors, environmental activists, and sports fishermen. The council itself has eleven members, six of whom can be described as "Alaskan," five as "from Outside." It is one of eight regional councils that devise the rules and catch quotas for the fisheries within 200 miles of the coast of the United States, essentially advising the U.S. Secretary of Commerce, who has the final say.

At the moment, the AP crab work group is trying to figure out how many tanner crab they think can be taken from the Bering Sea without endangering the ability of the stock to recover from what is apparently a low point in their biological cycle, which is itself something of a mystery. Their task is complicated because the crabbers catch the crab intentionally with pots, and the trawlers catch them accidentally when they are dragging for cod, sole, and other fish. When the work group members come up with the numbers describing what they consider to be a safe and fair amount, they will tell the council. The council will then either take or reject their advice and, in turn, advise the Secretary through the National Marine Fisheries Service. This process has been applied hundreds of times since passage of the Magnuson Fishery Conservation and Management Act of 1976, the key fisheries law of the land.

The discussions are difficult for outsiders to understand because a kind of subculture has evolved in the wake of the Magnuson Act. It has a new language, which includes such terms as allowable biological catch, optimum yield, incidental catch, and dozens of others, all of which have become part of an arcane code of acronyms: ABC, OY, IC, etc. These terms suffer from the implication that exact science is at work in this process; in fact, we know about as much about the oceans as we do about the moon, or so say most scientists who breathe the thin air of marine research. Nonetheless, decisions must be made.

This particular week-long meeting of the council—one of several held every year—is taking place in the Westward Hilton Hotel in Anchorage, Alaska. This year, 1986, is the first year that U.S. fleets will catch more in the waters off Alaska than foreign fleets, which, for a century, have held sway on those grounds.

The Players

The people who are deciding who gets what in these parts of the Pacific Ocean claimed by the United States are ordinary, save only for their connections to fisheries, management agencies, or state politics. And there they are, after a fifteen-minute break, hopping their chairs up to the long tables arranged in a big horseshoe against the wall of the ballroom. Long, vertical mirrors break the gold-flocked surface of the wall every few yards, lending an odd dance-hall tastelessness to the otherwise dignified room. The tables, on the other hand, are covered with white linen, and the inside of the horseshoe facing the audience is draped with what, to the hotel staff, is known as a "vanity shield." There is something unrefined, I suppose, about seeing the legs and feet of the council members. On the table in front of each of them or their seated advisors are a black-and-gold plastic pitcher, a glass, a microphone, a pile of papers, and three-ring binders.

The council chairman, Jim Campbell, is the owner of a building supply company in Anchorage and a close friend of the current governor of Alaska, Bill Sheffield. Campbell sits in the center of the horseshoe next to Jim Branson. Branson is the executive director of the council, a man whose experience in the fisheries of the North Pacific extends back more than a quarter-century to the days of virtually unenforceable treaties, full-on pirates, whaling, sealing, and a virtually cloistered management agency of insiders. He has no vote, but he has been the director of the council since 1976, when it was created, and has held his job through four chairmen: Elmer Rasmuson, '76–'77; Harold Lokken, '77–'78; Clement V. Tillion, '78–'83; and Campbell.

To the left and right of Campbell and Branson sit the members, four of whom do not vote. The voting members are Campbell; Don Collinsworth, commissioner of the Alaska Department of Fish and Game; Dr. John Donaldson, commissioner of the Oregon Department of Fish and Wildlife; Oscar Dyson, a fisherman from Kodiak; Sara Hemphill, a lawyer and owner of Alaska Contact Ltd., a firm that arranges fishing ventures with foreign fleets; Robert McVey, regional director of the Fisheries Service; Henry Mitchell, a lawyer and director of the Bering Sea Fishermen's Association; Rudy Peterson, a fisherman and fleet owner from Seattle; John Peterson, a seafood processor from Ocean Spray Seafoods; Bill Wilkerson, commissioner of the Washington Department of Fisheries; and John Winther, a fisherman from Petersburg, Alaska. The nonvoting members are Robert Gilmore, regional chief of the U.S. Fish and Wildlife Service; Dr. John Harville, director of the Pacific Marine Fisheries Commission; Rear Admiral Robert Lucas, U.S. Coast Guard district commander; and Stetson Tinkham, U.S. State Department.

The other participants in the Anchorage affair—"the people of the region," the Act calls us—occupy a battalion of chairs arranged in rule-straight chevrons angled toward the dais. The cast in the gallery changes from meeting to meeting and ranges in size from a few dozen to 400, depending on what is at stake. The cherished notion of public participation has produced testimony running from the obscure to the eloquent, and a cadre of regulars is essential to the process because they are the translators of the jargon, the decisions, and the political rhumba.

There, in the aquamarine upholstered chairs, are always people like Jay Hastings, a Seattle lawyer who works for Japanese fishing companies. He's been to virtually every meeting since the opening gun. Along the way he has borne endless stress and tension from his employers, who have been on the run since the Act passed, and from a lot of Americans who perceive him as nothing more than a traitor. He almost always looks tired, but never wrinkled despite his pool-hall slouch from hours and hours in the chairs. He's known for taking great notes. Then there's John Durkin, who usually watches quietly from one of the back rows, but who considers most of what goes on to be moot in the face of what he believes are illegal covenants that violate the rights of Alaska Natives and others who have fallen victim to international conspiracies after World War II. And then there's Chris Blackburn in her red go-to-meeting dress. From Kodiak, she's been writing about fish for years in newspapers all over the place but is now a professional watcher for a group of Alaska trawlers.

A lot of people who go to council meetings are professional watchers, for want of a better term. Some call them "the travelers," as in "Oh, you're the new traveler for the trollers." They're hired by groups of fishermen to travel to the steady stream of meetings that characterize the fishing business these days. Until just ten years ago, fishing in the

North Pacific was the exclusive purview of the last of the hunters of wild animals for food, and a meeting room is still the functional equivalent of a jail cell for most of them. The strain shows on the fishermen who are there. After the meetings, you'll find a fair knot of them in the hotel bars clutching their drinks as if they're the ejection seat handles of flaming jet fighters.

Without a traveler, a fishermen's group runs the risk of missing something that could quite literally put them out of business. Now, nobody in the government or the council intentionally hides anything in the corners of these proceedings, but it happens. Take, for instance, the agenda for this meeting.

What's at Stake?

At first glance, the list of topics doesn't look terribly consequential; most of the issues seem to be at that odd stage best described as irresolute discussion. The council approved a tanner crab incidental catch cap of such-and-such after the AP and the Scientific and Statistical Committee recommended such-and-such. Or, the council asked its Committee on the Reauthorization of the Act to continue its deliberations. Or, the council discussed joint management of crab with the Alaska Board of Fisheries. Or, the council members were asked to submit their evaluations of the council process in general. Business as usual, purely routine.

In translation, however, the deal that's going down should keep fishermen awake nights. As one crabber who was milling around in the lobby during a break put it, "These meetings all run together, but you've got to pay attention now. They're in there playing with the black chips this time." (In casinos, black chips are worth the most money.)

Consider the following: every confrontation between trawlers and crabbers—such as the one at the AP session earlier in this story— crackles with the wicked smell of the gear confrontation nightmare. For ten years, the council has been able to sidestep this one because foreign trawlers are usually dead meat in conflicts with American fishermen in this part of the world, so they just ruled against the foreigners every time. Now, though, it's Americans vs. Americans, and for one thing, they're a lot quicker on the lawsuit trigger than the foreigners, who tended to cower under the diplomatic hammer. Clearly, fixed gear (longlines and pots) is incompatible in a lot of fisheries with mobile gear (trawls); due compromise is called for. And the crabbers (fixed gear) are also tuning in to the habitat issues raised by the gear conflict with trawlers. Bottom trawling is like towing a pair of D–9 Cats linked by the anchor chain of the *Queen Mary* across the ocean floor.

But then there's the fact that industrial fleets have been catching a couple of million tons with bottom trawls for thirty years. "They're trashing our crab" . . . "No, we're not" . . . "Yes, you are" . . . "No, we're not" . . . is the street-fight version of the debate, usually accompanied by scientists hired by both sides, who contradict each other.

And check into the item on the agenda that reads "Legislative Update." This report by the council's Committee on the Reauthorization of the Act contains a sleeper, too. A group of processors has pitched for council support for a phase-out program to move the foreign fleets out of the U.S. zone by a specific date. The Act must be reauthorized—that is, amended and funded to reflect current wisdom and politics—and the bill to do that is currently stuck because one big hitter in the Senate wants it one way and another one wants something else. Their constituents have educated them on their interests, made the usual cash contributions, and the council must be the peacemaker.

Minutes after the legislative update simmers to the top of the pot, Chairman Campbell assigns further discussion to a special meeting in the evening to allow public testimony. The debate will be fueled by sentiments analogous to two tractor trailers, loaded with livestock and on a collision course, locking up brakes at ninety miles an hour: Alaska fleets vs. Seattle fleets; fishermen vs. processors. The same old story. The evening meeting, though, will run into the darkest part of the late-winter Alaskan night and produce some of the most eloquent orations ever presented to the council. Fishermen, lawyers, processors, and travelers will rise to the occasion like brook trout to the biggest mayfly they've ever seen. (But more on this later.)

That's another thing. These meetings go on and on and on and on, with little if any flagging of enthusiasm. The people around the council are acutely aware that they're playing in the big game, and that fact invigorates them. The hours they keep during a meeting could dry up the No-Doz market.

Another hunk of carbon angst will crackle into diamonds in a hot debate over the precious rights claimed by the state and federal governments over control of marine resources. This one is tucked into another innocuous agenda item: "Tanner Crab Management Plan." The winter before, the tanner crab season around Kodiak was open a week longer than it should have been to protect the stocks because the feds lacked the legal mechanism to close it quickly enough when the quota was reached unexpectedly fast. The two governments now manage the fish jointly in an uneasy alliance known as a "Memorandum of Agreement," but Alaskan fishermen would like nothing better than to see the appointed officials they control running things—that is, the Alaska Board of Fisheries. The fleet from Seattle, of course, would like nothing better than to take control themselves via the council.

And finally, buried in the backwater of the agenda, there is the matter of whether access to the grounds will remain open, as it has for hundreds of years. Two members of the council, John Peterson and John Harville, are on a commission formed by National Oceanic and Atmospheric Administration director Tony Calio to consider the council process, limiting access, and the broader strokes of American fisheries policy. Embedded in the charge to the commission is a brief but powerful policy evaluation by the Heritage Foundation, a conservative think tank, submitted to the Reagan administration in 1981 and updated in 1984. Essentially, the foundation recommends that the president replace the notion that the American seas are common property—that is open to all—with a system of private ownership. If the

American people own the resources in the sea, and the government represents the people, then the government should sell—not give away—those resources to the highest bidders, as is the case with oil leases, for instance.

All of the members of the council have been asked to give their opinions on the current management process to Harville and Peterson, who will pass them on to the Calio commission. The fidgeting stops when this one comes up.

Listening In

Kenny B. Bettisworth has never missed a meeting of the North Pacific Fishery Management Council. He's the compact man with a mustache at the end of the front row, dressed casually in slacks and a sweater. Hardly anybody knows who he is, though his face probably pops up often enough in nameless recognition among the denizens of the fish politics circuit. He's from an old Alaska family, from Fairbanks, I think, and has held the contract to tape-record the council meetings for ten years now. He is perfectly suited for the job, blessed with a nonchalance that allows him to say he has absolutely zero interest in the proceedings without insulting everybody in the fish business, to whom a council meeting can mean a fortune or ruin. "All I do is eat the fish," says Kenny, the ultimate consumer.

At the moment, the council is in what they call an open executive session, with no public testimony, hearing reports from various committees. Council director Jim Branson discusses the fiscal uncertainties that have arisen as the Gramm-Rudman-Hollings Act casts its long shadow over every cranny of the federal bureaucracy. Then he and the staff deliver updates on topics ranging from the high-seas salmon treaty with Japan to the status of several management plans, work groups, and special committees. It's all a steady, boring drone until newspapers rustle and vinyl seats creak when he gets to the issue of the reauthorization of the Magnuson Act. The House bill to carry on and finance the implementation of the Act, which expires this year, happens to be stalled in the Senate, partly because the various factions are lined up behind disparate versions.

One version, with Alaska Senator Ted Stevens at the helm, proposes that an early specific date be set for eliminating foreign fleets from the zone. He wants that included in the reauthorization bill. The other camp, led by Washington Senator Slade Gorton, claims that the phase-out is under way already and running just fine and that we don't need to bust the chops of our foreign joint-venture partners when they're on the way out anyway. Naturally, their respective constituencies of fishermen stand to gain or lose depending on which way the deal goes down.

Special Committee, Sleight of Hand

Judiciously, Campbell orders the issue tabled and convenes a meeting of the special reauthorization committee for that evening at seven-thirty. A few ritual groans emanate from the gallery, but the council's reputation for working hard has been earned at night meetings that add three or four hours to days that begin for most members and interested parties with the 8:00 a.m. opening gavel. Kenny Bettisworth asks if the night session has to be taped, and Campbell tells him no. Only the main meetings of the council must be recorded. Kenny smiles and takes a hit off his cigarette. It's all just noise to him.

That noise, though, comes from the people who, in one combination or another, will inherit the North Pacific grounds off Alaska. That year, 1986, marked the first time that U.S. fishermen caught more in the Gulf of Alaska and Bering Sea than the foreigners. That means conflicts among the American fleets—trawlers, longliners, crabbers, and the rest—are intensifying, as are those between fishermen and processors, and those between fishermen from Alaska and those from elsewhere. Naturally, with the dice rolling, everybody wants their own numbers to come up.

Four centuries ago, when humans moved to be near food, the volcanic Aleutian Chain, which cleaves the North Pacific, was one of the most populous regions on Earth. Today, the Aleutian Islands are sparsely settled, and we ship food around the world from the waters around them, and the fertile grounds draw fishermen from around the world. For the past twenty-five years, international fleets of trawlers, longliners, and pot boats have been taking something like 6 billion pounds of seafood a year from the Bering Sea and Gulf of Alaska. That includes pollock; Pacific cod; Atka mackerel; king, tanner, and hair crab; halibut; salmon; ocean perch; rockfish; sole; and black cod. Well over 90 percent of the historical catch has been landed in foreign ports. When the American fleets take over, though, their catch will more than double the total U.S. landings (1984) of edible seafood.

We are talking here about very big money, somewhere on the order of $4 billion to $5 billion in the first level of trade alone. "All you have to do to make a lot of money is to get a small piece of something very big," advised an obscure Los Angeles auto-wrecking genius twenty years ago.

With the squall of new investment waiting in the wings to develop the U.S. fleet comes political pressure on the Magnuson Act. Tucked deeply in the folds of the reauthorization process are considerations of the council structure (which gets pretty good grades this time around) and even the notion of the fishing grounds as an open-access, common-property resource. Council members John Peterson, who is a packing company executive in his spare time, and Dr. John Harville, who's from Oregon, are members of the ad hoc commission thinking about such revolutionary propositions.

"We are charged with defining the role of the federal government in the fisheries," Peterson reports to the council in Anchorage. "We have been asked for our opinion as to who should pay for such management and asked to analyze the concept of common property as it applies to fisheries. Calio told us to analyze these things free from the constraints of existing laws or institutions."

The genesis of Calio's inquiry into the way we do business in the fish trade lies in the very fabric of the conservative economic theory that now dominates federal thought in America. "We should learn from the 'tragedy of the commons' paradigm," Fred Singer told the council. He's an administrative advisor whose observations on American fisheries were included in "Agenda '83," published by the Heritage Foundation, a conservative think tank.

Goats, apparently, gave the "tragedy of the commons" author his clue. "Free access to a common grazing meadow encourages each herder to increase the size of his herd and eventually destroys the resource base through over-grazing," Singer wrote. "We should sell property rights to fishing grounds within the U.S. Fishery Conservation Zone."

And in an article he wrote for the *Wall Street Journal* in 1985, Singer—whose theories and advice are highly regarded by the Reagan revolution—said, "The Act has been administered as if the resource belonged to the fishermen, in that U.S. fishermen are charged nothing for the right to fish. But, as with offshore oil and gas, the resource should be considered the property of all U.S. citizens. Imagine the storm of protest if oil and gas worth $2.4 billion [one estimate of U.S. zone landings] were given away to energy companies every year!" (Singer conveniently ignores the oil depletion tax allowance, which effectively does just that.) He went on to say that any federal price support for the fishing industry should immediately be eliminated in favor of giving rise to the ownership-enterprise formula.

Stunning Ignorance

Singer's remarks didn't get a lot of ink, but people with an interest in the fishing business who happened to hear what he said started foaming at the mouth. Alaska Congressman Don Young, a Republican, wrote the Heritage Foundation a long letter, which he read into the *Congressional Record* of February 8, 1983. It says, in part, "I recently received a copy of 'Agenda '83' and found it to be full of many excellent suggestions for the reform of our government and government policies . . . While I'm sure Dr. Singer is a competent environmental scientist, he appears to have written the article in a vacuum; the article demonstrates his stunning ignorance of the political and economic realities within which the U.S. fishing industry must operate."

Young's letter goes on for several hundred words, suggesting that Singer look at price supports in other industries, correct technical errors in his theories, refrain from comparing a nonrenewable, nonmobile resource such as oil to a renewable, movable resource such as fish, and quit touting limited entry as a means to increase economic efficiency. "In sum," Young concludes, "I think that Dr. Singer has completely ignored the realities of the fishing industry to promote an economist's utopia."

Some splendid philosophical arguments have grown from Singer's seeds, and during the break after Peterson and Harville gave their report on their work with the Calio commission, the lobby chatter is particularly high-pitched. Later, though, at the night session of the reauthorization committee, the complexities of economic theory and special-interest politics give way to the more immediate matter of replacing foreign fleets with American fleets.

Under committee chairman Don Collinsworth, eight people testify in three hours; the committee members ask questions. The short version is: Phasing out the foreign fleets is dicey because some people, mainly joint-venture fishermen doing business with the Russians, Japanese, and Koreans, are very dependent on them as they seek their fortunes. Others, mainly processors, say they can't do business with the foreigners in the picture. It is, quite simply, a major policy collision between strong factions.

The matter has arisen at the council meeting because the Pacific Seafood Processors' Association wrote a letter to Chairman Campbell suggesting that the council adopt three measures as part of its Magnuson Act reauthorization package: (1) end all foreign fishing in the U.S. zone by 1988; (2) set specific percentages of the total catch that may be taken by joint ventures in which U.S. catcher boats deliver to foreign factory vessels; and (3) recognize the existing tier system in the Act, which gives top priority to American processors when making allocations.

Stating the Case

Generally (and there are many exceptions), setting a certain date for running the foreign fleets off the grounds sets up a conflict between the traditionally polarized elements of the North Pacific fisheries: Seattle (against setting the date) vs. Alaska (for); fishermen (against) vs. processors (for). Here's how some of them sound this night in Anchorage when Kenny Bettisworth and his tape recorder have the night off:

- Trefon Angasan, owner of the 125-foot trawler *Great Pacific*: "My trawling operation was managed for seven years by a salmon company, and it brought us to our knees. Now we're fishing for Taiyo [a Japanese company], and we're getting high tonnage and a fair price. We see joint ventures as an important part of Americanizing the grounds. We have twenty-year mortgages on boats that are finally making some money trawling. We need to continue joint ventures to make our payments."
- Don Collinsworth, council member and commissioner of the Alaska Department of Fish and Game: "Bankers like [date-certain] phase-out. They're all faced with a system that's full of vagaries, the way it goes up and down."
- Jay Hastings, representing Japanese fishing companies in the United States: "The people behind me are the best friends the U.S. fishing industry has. The processors' push to run them off the grounds is not based on analysis of the market or economics. They think phase-out will force the Japanese to buy from them. They are wrong. Taiyo and Nippon Suisan are not going to fall over dead if there is a date-certain

phase-out. I oppose a mechanical or legislated date-certain phase-out as compared to an economically driven phase-out. The Japanese have accepted the fact that they are on the way out since 1976."

- John Peterson, council member and seafood processor: "With regard to the Japanese who may be put out of work, better them than us. This is the whole thrust of the Magnuson Act."

- Larry Cotter, Alaska labor leader and Advisory Panel member: "The seafood-processing work force has the lowest income in the state of Alaska, less than $5,000 per year on the average. How do I explain to that work force that out of 5 billion pounds of seafood taken in the U.S. zone off Alaska, 4 billion pounds went to foreign processing fleets in direct foreign fishing and joint ventures?"

- Sara Hemphill, council member and joint-venture agent: "We've got more of an opportunity to milk the situation without a date-certain phase-out."

- Thorn Tasker, joint-venture boat owner and an Alaskan: "You talk about needing to provide an attractive investment environment, but that seems to be true about a date-certain phase-out only if you're a processor. Well, if you ignore the fishermen, you're doing a disservice to the people who built this industry."

The Night Wears On

Then Tasker gives voice to the sentiments of the crews aboard the boats at sea off Alaska on this late-winter night. "You want to bring up stuff like this, then I'll get the fishermen in here. Everything else you talk about is play school compared to what you'd get with a couple of hundred guys who are finally making a living out there fishing in joint ventures. If the letter from the processors' association is part of the council's reauthorization recommendation, we'll bring the fishermen in."

Other fishermen at the meeting speak, too, and their deep concern imparts an eloquence that would have caught the ear of even the most casual observers, had there been any in the mirrored ballroom this night. The gallery of fishermen, biologists, politicians, and travelers rustle like an edgy herd as two men from the Pacific Seafood Processors' Association stand up. Bob Brophy and Bob Morgan, who together have more years in the fish business than they'll admit to, walk purposefully down the aisle between the rows of chairs to defend their demand for setting a certain date for phasing out foreign fleets.

They're both big men, each well over six feet tall, and the chairs at the witness table seem barely able to contain them. Former salmon packer Morgan begins the by-now-familiar litany: "Mr. Chairman, members of the council . . .

"We're not suggesting that U.S. fishermen will get hurt; we simply want to replace foreign buyers with U.S. buyers. If they don't have access to the raw product forms, market access will follow."

Then fisherman and council member Oscar Dyson of Kodiak asks Morgan, "How many boats could your groups put to work right now, today?"

"Well, I don't know. I suppose our ships can produce as much as their ships," Morgan replies.

"We want to Americanize. We've been at it a long time," Dyson says.

Then Barry Fisher, a joint-venture pioneer, chimes in with: "Would you guys [Morgan and Brophy] agree that this is not simple, that this is a contentious issue?"

"Yes, but it's because we haven't explained our position well enough," says Morgan.

"Would you entertain the thought of coming back and joining a group to analyze markets and economics with us? Let's do it together," Fisher says, ever the conciliator.

"We've got to be concerned that the discussion doesn't go on forever," says Morgan. "This could be a tactic, not necessarily on your part, but it could be used by the foreigners."

"This is the most important issue the council will ever have to deal with. We have to set aside the time to work on it," Fisher says.

At this point, three hours into the night session with eleven o'clock coming 'round, John Peterson, who started the debate with his letter to the council, on behalf of the processors withdraws his request. Collinsworth forms a special phase-out committee and sets its first meeting six months into the next year.

"There are some very different economic interests at play here," Collinsworth says, bringing the meeting to a close with what everybody agrees is a classic understatement. "We will inevitably be asking people to compromise on their interests. It's going to be a tough process."

Too bad Kenny isn't here.

By 1990, all foreign fishing fleets in U.S. waters were banished, replaced by U.S.-flag boats delivering to shore plants and offshore factory ships. Most processing companies in the "Americanized" fleets, both ashore and off the coast, are financed with cash from Japan, Korea, Norway, and Denmark.

The North Pacific Fishery Management Council and the other seven that manage the nation's fisheries survived major changes in the Magnuson Act in 1996, after some speculation that the system would be dismantled. The councils were created, however, at a time when virtually all fisheries were in development mode and now have to make the transition to sustainability rather than continued growth. Every council now has an environmental activist or two on its advisory panel, and risk-averse management is on everyone's mind as we grapple with overfishing, excess bycatch, and deteriorating ocean and coastal habitat.

Flying Fish and the Death of a Plane at Egegik

SALMON SETNETTING ▪ BRISTOL BAY, 1985

I first heard about the DC–6 crash when I was standing around the coffee urn in the galley of a processing barge, not as interested in the thin coffee as in the jive and rumors that flow wherever fishing crews eat together. The galley of the *Bering Star* is an ingenious, miniature cafeteria with seats for fifty in a claustrophobic tangle of chrome-and-yellow-plastic tables. It is mug-up, a break from work when only a few people take the time to shuck their gory oilskins, as they must to enter the galley. Most grab their coffee from a cart on the processing deck and take it out on the catwalks that rise in tiers along the deep-blue sides of the barge.

The few visiting fishermen, tendermen, and off-shift workers who are in the galley are gathered around a guy wearing sweats and the most revolting, gurry-spattered baseball cap I've ever seen. I can barely make out the red Viking ship in a circle that is the logo of Icicle Seafoods. He's demonstrating his trick: he can breathe Jell-O. With a substantial red mound in a bowl on the table, he locks his hands behind his back, dips his head forward, and *schluppppppp*. Gone. That fast. He does it three times and everybody cheers.

The barge is at anchor off Clark's Point in the mouth of the Nushagak River on the west side of the Bay. Mothered by the strong, brown flow of the river, this spot is usually one of the most productive, but this season that part of the run is weak and nobody knows why. I hear the east side is crackling, though, with strong runs to the Ugashik and Egegik Rivers drawing most of the gillnetters, packers, and planes.

Bristol Bay is almost always called simply "the Bay," and only the greenest of North Pacific fishermen will be puzzled by the reference. It lies on the chart in the crotch between the pocked alluvial fan of the Yukon River and the volcanic Alaska Peninsula, which runs west to the nether world of the Aleutian Chain. For eight weeks every year, upwards of 40 million red salmon rush through the distant passes of the Chain into the Bering Sea and then to Bristol Bay. There, they merge with 30,000 fishermen, packers, pilots, and hustlers in the biggest spawning frenzy on the planet.

So anyway, during the Jell-O sucking, this woman with dark hair, high-mileage eyes, and a red tee-shirt comes up to me there in the galley of the *Bering Star* and draws her own cup of watery coffee. She's the cook. We watch the performance, and after a couple of minutes of "whaddya doing up here on the Bay," she asks me if I heard about the big plane crash. It involved, she said, a four-engine DC–6 freighter, fifteen tons of salmon, the Moonies, and a forty-foot bluff on the lee edge of the beach at Egegik. A real disaster, but the Bay is always dangerous. A renegade thought momentarily pulls my mind to another lee shore where, almost thirty-seven years ago to the day, on July 5, 1948, twenty-six men died when a northerly breeze backed around, became a southerly gale, and beat their brave little sailboats to pulp in a rising tide on Deadman Sands. Not long after, in 1951, engine power was made legal on the Bay, leaving only the elegant Chesapeake Bay oyster fleet under mandatory sail.

That remembrance is just a synaptic flash, a moment's pause, but it becomes a whole thought in that instant. I realize that the most vicious of uncertainties—once the companions of the fishermen of the sailing fleet—arc now flying co-pilot in a new age. To be sure, the sea will always roar in dark, deadly patterns, but the airplane crash has become the modern incarnation of mortal risk there on Bristol Bay. Instead of talking about the DC–6, we sip our coffee, a simultaneous gesture like a nervous tic; the silence is not awkward. I ask her how many people died in the crash. Her shoulders rise and sag as the topic is acknowledged to be mortality.

"Oh, I hear two," she says. "But I don't know for sure. Poor things."

We don't mention the plane again, our conversation taking its usual turns through personal history, the size of the salmon run, money, boredom, and her philosophic vision of Bristol Bay as a home for lost boys and girls who refuse to grow up, who crave the single-minded pursuit of fishing out here because it brings a revitalizing kind of irresponsibility and freedom to life. Cooks on fishing boats and processing ships are like bass players in jazz bands; they keep the beat while everybody else improvises. The next day, another cook in another galley would tell me there were four aboard the DC–6 and that he didn't think there were any survivors.

At that point, an odd compulsion began to overtake me despite my reason for being on the Bay, which was to cover the fishing. It would eventually lead me to a scrap pile of wrecked airplane and smoking meat on a remote Arctic beach, after winding a twisted course through permanent truths that, somehow, would prove false. I had been to the Bay before, insulated in the protective wrapping of a journalist, but this time would be different.

Toward Egegik

I fled the processing barge and its inhabitants suffering under the lash of sixteen-hour shifts and bad coffee for a chance to get to the east side aboard the packer *Viking Queen*. I had met her skipper, Kari Toivolo, in the galley of the *Bering Star* while his crew was unloading. I learn that he is a twenty-six-year-old Finlander, that he's been running the *Viking Queen* for four years, that he put in his deck time aboard her during the glory days of king crab. The old-timers on the Bay tend to get more notice than the kids because fishing is a business that celebrates and rewards longevity, but king crab and the other high-bucks booms brought a fresh generation up through the ranks more quickly than usual. Many were very young when they went to sea to pick pots or run gear, tough kids in the new athletic fisheries that, more than ever before, paid well for youth's endurance and courage. Now, a man or woman of twenty-six can easily have ten years' experience as a fisherman or mariner, and many are running big boats or packing operations.

When Kari offers me a ride to the east side I accept without hesitation because I am drawn to the action and already in the tingling grip of curiosity about the DC–6 on Egegik Beach. And then there's the fact that a good salmon tender like the *Viking Queen* is almost a yacht, and I cannot turn down that kind of comfort on the water. The *Viking Queen* is a solid, ninety-two-foot, steel-hulled packer/crabber, one of ten built during the sixties at the Pacific Fishermen Yard in Seattle. She is a schooner, with an after-house, high whale-back bows, and plenty of room in between for three tanked holds chilled by a refrigerated seawater system.

Under way, the view from the bridge over the planked expanse of her deck is a visual mantra as we roll in waltz time across Bristol Bay, a pure example of the calming embrace of a gentle sea. Thought becomes a matter of harmony rather than details, a collection of images much too big to be carried by a fellow like me under ordinary circumstances. It happens to be Kari's wheelwatch as we pull away from the barge, and he sits silently across the bridge to my right. The constant conversation of meeting has fallen off now, and the only sound breaking the bubble of the grumbling engines comes when the young skipper reaches up every few minutes to adjust his autopilot. The Iron Mike responds with a series of ratchety clicks. I let my mind wander through the history of the Bay, with a piece of that history there under my boots and an heir to the tradition a few feet away in the captain's chair. Over the short span of a couple of generations, packing salmon from the Earth's most prolific run has been transformed from a primitive, feudalistic, food-gathering frenzy that was dependent on cheap labor, to a breakneck dash featuring big money, fast boats, and airplanes.

Looking Back

The *VQ*, as the *Viking Queen* is familiarly known, is owned by Icicle Seafoods, a company started thirty years ago by a few fishermen in Petersburg, Alaska, when the only processor in town closed its doors. They parlayed their instincts, energy, and a small packing plant into some good money. The money got very large in the late seventies when the Americans, with a stroke of the pen that signed the Magnuson Act, shut the Japanese out of the salmon, herring, and king crab grounds of the Bering Sea within 200 miles of the coast. That meant they had to buy salmon, herring, and crab for their hungry markets, and guess who was selling?

Naturally, the Japanese wanted to ensure dependable supplies, so they invested heavily in American processing companies and triggered a nauseating wave of xenophobia. Japanese investments made for great debates in the bars and fishing trade papers, though. Some Americans, particularly Alaskans, who are very allergic to absentee ownership of anything, raved about Japanese control of their industry. Others pointed out that the Asian buyers were simply good customers, so what's the problem? The truth, as usual, is somewhere in between. In search of that truth, the state of Alaska commissioned a study on Japanese ownership that only confused things further because the researchers were never able to penetrate the veils of interlocking directorates that are common in Japanese industry. The charts in the report showing the flow of corporate investment looked about as meaningful as the stains left on the wrappings of a noodle lunch.

Nowhere was the Japanese outburst of investment of 1978 to 1981 felt more than on Bristol Bay, where, for almost a century, business as usual had meant tightly held, family fish-packing fiefdoms with highly dependent fleets of fishermen. For millennia, the salmon of the Bay had nourished the seasonally migrant Eskimos, Aleuts, and watershed Indians. The incursion into those ancient patterns and places by the American square-rigger fleets in the early part of this century established an order that remained essentially undisturbed until the Japanese buying frenzy arrived.

Of course, the technology and conditions changed over these years. During the square-rigger era, the ships would load lumber, cans, dories, fishermen, and Asian laborers in San Francisco and Seattle, sail north through Unimak Pass into the Bering Sea, and then head up into the funnel of Bristol Bay. There, the ships would anchor off their canneries, the captains would become superintendents, the fishermen fished, and the laborers canned the salmon. When they had a shipload, the laborers and fishermen would board up the canneries, pack the ships, and sail south with the goods. It was an efficient, though autocratic, proposition.

The square-riggers gave way to steam, and the sail-and-oar-powered dories went in 1951 when engines became legal. (Managers of the era believed that restricting fishermen to sail power was an effective tool to limit their catch.) That really was the beginning of the end for the old order. The engines made the fishermen far less dependent on the canneries, even though they remained employees and their boats were owned outright by the fish companies until the late 1950s. The harbinger of the next era of the independent fisherman was the *Judy*

Joyce, a tidy thirty-two-foot gillnetter that, in 1985, was still fishing, though somewhat ceremonially. She was the first boat on the Bay ever owned by a fisherman, financed by Winn Brindle, patriarch of the powerful Red Salmon Company.

For another twenty-five years, through lean seasons while the Japanese fleets were slugging the salmon on the high seas and the inshore runs were weak, the fishermen remained little more than chattel of the packing companies. The canneries bought the fish but did very little negotiating on the price. (Virtually every fish went into a can.) They sold the fishermen food, fuel, and rooms in bunkhouses on shore and controlled the supply side of their marketing equation by placing their fishermen on limits when the runs were strong so as not to exceed demand. For canning companies such as Red Salmon, New England Fish, Whitney Fidalgo, and dozens of others, it was still Fat City.

In many cases, the arrangement between fishermen and packers was mutually benevolent, but abuses were common and the patterns of mistrust that took root remain today. After fishermen became "independent businessmen" in the late fifties, they formed a pair of hybrid unions: the Alaska Independent Fishermen's Marketing Association (AIFMA), based in Naknek on the east side of the Bay, and the Western Alaska Cooperative Marketing Association in Dillingham on the west side. The unions were technically hybrids because the courts had ruled that since each fisherman was essentially an independent business, they could only meet to discuss prices before negotiation with the canneries under special rules or they would be in violation of antitrust laws. Fishermen always complained that they were unfairly restrained while the canneries routinely colluded on the price.

AIFMA was the larger group, formed around a nucleus of fishermen of Portuguese, Italian, and Serbo-Croatian ancestry from California who were the heirs of the square-rigger tradition. Sometimes the bunkhouses sounded like a United Nations barbecue, and translators were necessary during negotiations. WACMA represented mostly local, native Alaskan fishermen, but they pretty much went along with the AIFMA line. Until 1980, the fishermen of the Bay wielded their power and independence in relatively straightforward ways. Every season, individual packers offered a price for reds, chums, kings, silvers, and pinks. Reds were the real money fish, and settlements for the others were always easy. The fishermen either accepted the red price or began a period of toe-to-toe negotiations prodded by the certain and imminent return of the run, which usually begins during the last week of June and peaks around July 10.

The fishermen's bargaining position gained considerable strength in 1974 when Alaska passed a law limiting the number of permits that would be issued to fish on the Bay to about 1,750. That meant the fishermen could enter negotiations with no fear at all that the canneries would hire scabs to take their places if they decided to strike.

Changes in the Wind

When the old order was finally displaced in 1980, Icicle Seafoods both literally and symbolically administered the coup de grâce. In 1978, the energetic little company from Petersburg slipped on a new set of financial pajamas and climbed in bed with Mitsubishi and Hoei Trading, major Japanese trading companies that approach their ventures like Godzilla devouring Yokohama. Icicle's main deal with Mitsubishi was a stroke of genius. Their Japanese partners and buyers financed two big, efficient processor-freezer barges—the *Bering Star* and *Arctic Star*—that Icicle could move among the herring, salmon, and crab fisheries. In return, Mitsubishi and its various subsidiaries got the rights of first refusal on the seafood. They could also tell Icicle just how they wanted it handled and packed and, with Icicle's several shore plants also going full steam, guarantee themselves a solid market share. Some canneries scrambled to install freezers in their shore plants. Floaters had been the coming thing, though, since the late fifties when Augie Mardesich came to the Bay with his primitive processor-freezer

North Star, formerly Admiral Byrd's flagship. But nobody got it quite right until Icicle and the Star Fleet.

When the Icicle floaters arrived on the Bay, the old-line packers and fishermen regarded them as maritime incarnations of the Empire Death Star of *Star Wars* fame. What kind of services would these interlopers provide for fishermen, they scoffed. Where were the bunkhouses, showers, and mess halls that had turned the Bay into a kind of summer camp for fifty years? What kind of guarantees they'd be around next season? Who are these guys, anyway? Nothing but a front for the Japanese. They're nothing but glorified fly-by-night cash buyers. Who loves you, baby?

But the Icicle Deathbarges and another similar rig, Nelbro Packing Company's *Ultra Processor,* coincided with the arrival of a new kind of fishing boat on the Bay. Although the state limits Bristol Bay drift gillnet boats to thirty-two feet in length, the day boats of the old cannery regime were being replaced by glass or aluminum numbers featuring full galleys and berthing for round-the-clock crews. These big boats cost anywhere from $60,000 to $300,000, but the money was there and with one of them, a Bristol Bay gillnetter was finally really independent. No longer did he need a shore plant to call home during the season. He could also run the coast for other fisheries, such as herring, if he had the permits, and his packing plant could go with him. Icicle, its partners, and emulators had it figured.

In 1980, the Deathbarges and their mobile, independent fleets of modern gillnetters, many of whom were highliners from Icicle's home grounds in Southeast Alaska, met head to head with the 48 Talls, as the packers of the old order were called. When the cannery fishermen tied up to wait for a better price and fired up their barbecues, the Icicle fishermen ignored the strike and went fishing. In the past, an AIFMA strike had been observed by virtually all fishermen on the Bay, either out of sympathy or in fear of reprisals (which were not unheard of) by striking fishermen. In 1980, the "scabs" of the Icicle fleet were joined by 200 to 300 other fishermen who sold to other floaters and cash buyers anchored in the Bay. The docks at Naknek and Dillingham rumbled with threats. Ugly, serious fights broke out at the Sea Inn, Hadfield's, Fishermen's, and the other bars. There had always been fights, but never like these.

With the clarity of hindsight, it's obvious that the Bay in 1980 was in the midst of cataclysmic change, that nothing would ever be "the same" again. High prices, enormous post-200-mile-limit red runs, and modern freezer technology combined to alter the entire character of the old soup. A lot of people didn't care for the flavor when the bankers, lawyers, and MBAs started doing the stirring, with recipes from the Asian joint-venture partners. It was a nasty time.

High Prices and Airplanes

The 48 Talls had grown dominant in an era when getting experience extracted deadly costs in lives and money. Newcomers had to be wrong, they thought. But the high prices and vigorous Japanese competition meant there was still room for cleverness on one other potentially profitable front: transportation. If the wholesale price of red salmon jumps 400 percent in one year as it did in 1980, the fish can stand a lot of added value, but mainly in that one critical area. For the first time, the price was high enough to support shipping salmon by air to other freezer plants, canneries, and even directly to market.

Designer salmon struck another sour note for the 48 Talls who had built their companies and fortunes on canning. They steadfastly refused to believe that the sands were shifting. "Tin built the Bay," was the war cry during the strike of 1980, "and tin will keep it strong." But cans were invented for storing food for long periods. Some guy in the nineteenth century figured out how to can food for Napoleon so he could feed his armies. The emperor's field kitchens were not in line for any *prix de cuisine*, but that it was edible was enough; taste really didn't matter. To be sure, the canned salmon coming out of Alaska was probably the best canned fish you could buy anywhere in the world, and it had been a staple in many homes for years. But it's still canned fish, and it just isn't as good to eat as a well-frozen salmon. There was no way that the future of Bristol Bay would be built on tin, not if it was wrapped around salmon that cost a processor a dollar a pound at the dock.

". . . So, you falling asleep over there?" It's Kari Toivolo. "I guess I'm keeping you up." His bridge routine has brought him to consideration of the stranger, and now we talk again for a while. Soon, his wheel-watch ends and he retires for a nap, telling his relief to call him before we reach the anchorage at the mouth of the Ugashik River. I go below, too, to the galley, where I find the rest of the crew sleeping through the eight-hour run. When they're buying fish, sleep is rare, so now's the time. I decide to grab a few hours myself and twist into an upper bunk.

I grow restless in the tight confines and careen from the peace of the *Viking Queen* under way to visions of the last moments of the DC–6 at Egegik. What did it look like? The version in my mind's eye is built with scraps of fear from other plane crashes I'd seen and heard of on the Bay. Like the midair over the beach on the west bank in 1981 that took Sumner Putman, Federico DeLaurentis, and one of the pilots from Texas who had come up with his family and seemed to be having such a good time out here. Then there was the C–119 at Egegik in 1981 that hit on the flats a mile from shore just at dusk, and nobody could get to the crew, who were crying out for help. Only after one of them fell into the water did they find out it was only shoulder-deep and they were in no danger of drowning, at least for a while. They were rescued.

Horizontal paradise overtakes me and I doze off.

In the Ugashik

After what seems like only seconds, the cook wakes me and says we are in the Ugashik River. I stumble from the stateroom and, just as I reach the after-rail for a breath of air, a red-and-white Cessna 180 on floats taxies up to the *Viking Queen*.

"Can we get fuel?" the pilot shouts over the engine noise from his perch on his portside pontoon.

"Come alongside," Kari yells out the wheelhouse window, and the plane noses gingerly up to our starboard rail. The pilot is a spotter, hired by a syndicate of Icicle fishermen to fly over the Bay and look for hot spots, revealed by either swarms of salmon near the surface or other fishermen hauling back heavy nets. When he finds one, he radios his fishermen, who gain a competitive edge with such information. In the crowded skies over the Bering Sea, the spotter has one of the deadliest jobs in the world, short of combat in war. Some die every year.

"The problem," the pilot says, ignoring the obvious, "is that pretty soon everybody's going to be watching everybody else, and it'll be like a big dog chasing its own tail out there."

I ask him what he knows about the Egegik crash, and he tells me everybody was saved. He's not sure how many people were aboard, but the Moonies from their fish camp and some old guy with a chain saw were the heroes. The wreckage burned hot and is still smoking, he says, a black scar against the bluff.

For forty-eight hours, the *VQ* is in the Ugashik buying salmon. The familiar rhythms of fish tendering destroy time as the deckhands work 'round the clock and the gillnetters filter into the river from the flats with the news that the fishing is just okay. The protocol on the salmon grounds calls for the boat crews to unload the fish while the skippers come aboard the tender to check weights, sign fish tickets, place orders for food and parts, and gossip with the tender captain. Kari mans his station at a ledger desk in the forepeak.

Kari is the agent for the fish company, responsible for this first link in the chain of commerce that brings salmon to tables around the world.

As is also the custom, Kari and the company offer the fishing skipper a small gift with each delivery, a vestigial token acknowledging loyalty, usually a six-pack of beer.

At night, the scene intensifies under sharp halogen glow. Gillnetters appear suddenly alongside as they break into the ring of light, lurching apparitions festooned with orange and pink buoy balls, their crews in orange and yellow slickers rescued from comedy by the dead-tired expressions on their faces and the gunning of powerful engines. As the tender rolls, the light from the masthead is cast farther away from us to illuminate other boats waiting in the shadows, bobbing violently in the choppy flow of the river. At night, the mortal danger of the Bay grows more apparent.

Bound for Egegik

Finally, later on our second day in the Ugashik, Kari is ordered to sail and to deliver his salmon to the processing barge *Arctic Star*, sister to the *Bering Star*, anchored off the Naknek River to the east. It's about an eight-hour run from the Ugashik, and I'm elated. From Naknek, I can easily make my way to King Salmon airport, just ten miles away, and from there catch a plane to Egegik Beach. The certainty that I am going where I want to go is an anesthetic, and I sleep all the way to Naknek. There, I wake for thanks and good-byes to the crew of the *Viking Queen* and hitch a ride with a shore-bound tender.

Hitchhiking by sea, road, or air is an easy proposition on the Bay, and a day after reaching Naknek, I'm wedged into the tail cone of a single-engine Cessna 206 bound for Egegik Beach. The airport at King Salmon seemed calm compared with past years when the price of fish was so high that flying them out was a bargain. This season, there are fewer planes, and the activity on the ramps seems more organized than the circuses they became from 1980 to 1984. By the 1985 season, after four years of attrition due to economics and fatalities, the survivors of the air war on the Bay have the deal pretty well figured out. Most of the flying museum pieces—the C–119s, Boeing Stratoclippers, and C–124s—are gone, and the labor intensity that characterized the beginnings of the salmon-flying era has evolved into a coterie of veteran outfits such as Northern Air Cargo, Winky's Peninsula Seafoods, and Ball Brothers. Newcomers are less likely to take the plunge when faced with well-drilled competition that can accomplish such feats as picking up 30,000 pounds of salmon from a beach and flying it 500 miles, three times a day.

For freelance pilots and adventurous brokers, the end of the old order on the Bay, whatever its cause, was an opportunity to be seized. Speed is stock and trade if you're buying fresh fish, and that's what the airplanes brought to the Bay in the new age. When you're moving red salmon that wholesales for $3.50 a pound, you can just about buy the stuff a first-class seat and still make wicked good money. According to several sources who were in on the volatile early years of the Japanese frozen salmon action and collapse of the 48 Tall canners, all you had to do was get the fish away from the Bay and into cold storage and then hang on. In 1980, the price of red salmon went from $.50 a pound to $2.10 a pound in three months. If you didn't have to borrow money at runaway interest rates to keep control of your fish, you made a killing. That kind of situation presented itself over and over again.

And for that special tribe of people who live and breathe flight, Bristol Bay in the early eighties was a combination meal ticket and free pass to aviation-junkie heaven. The ramp at the King Salmon airport was nothing short of a museum, with flying exhibits ranging from crop dusters to antique transports, such as those double-decker Stratoclippers that were essentially passenger versions of the B–29 and, of course, the crown jewel of the four-engine, piston airliners, the DC–6. And there was no shortage of modern equipment. Chartered jets with uniformed crews are routine on the ramp during the season. The DC–8 and 727 jets bear the colors of cargo lines you've never heard of unless you've been around a Third World war zone or read a lot of aviation mags.

Playing the Odds

The planes operate under the same rules out here on the edge of the world that apply everyplace else, but the amount of traffic and the vast areas of uncontrolled airspace make the Bay a statistical nightmare for pilots. Forget instrument approaches with virtually 100 percent certainty that you'll make it. Here, you roll the dice with maybe 80 percent certainty, or even 60 percent when you're taking off in soft sand, 500 pounds over gross and tail-heavy into zero wind except for the killer downdrafts from the bluff just thirty feet off your left wing tip. Another problem is congestion—just too many planes and choppers in the air at the same time. Generally, the pilots are okay, but you also have a bunch of hobbyists and flat-out flakes flying around up there, too. And that's the rub. Fatal crashes are not rare, with midair collisions leading the parade.

Nevertheless, the big flying fish packers are life symbols, dramatic evidence that commerce is under way, that food is getting to market, that the money is rolling in. The airplanes on the Bay are kin to the giant, near-mythic 747s and space shuttles. Like the magnificent square-riggers and steamships of the last age, they draw crowds to the spectacles of their comings and goings, somehow offering the people who come powerful reassurances that humankind is succeeding. A crash, particularly of a big airplane, is a serious threat to order, shredding those reassurances.

Our first approach to Egegik in the 206 that day is a failure. From my place on piles of gear in the windowless tail of the plane, I can see nothing without straining forward, and then my view outside is obscured anyway. Low fog blankets the beach, and though the ground winks up through a few sucker holes, none is large enough for landing. The pilot, a fellow from Arizona up for the season with his new wife, wisely decides to return to King Salmon. And there we wait for six hours, drinking coffee and watching the ground crew at Winky Crawford's Peninsula Seafoods, a.k.a. the Flying Circus. They are an odd assortment of characters, a cross between barnstormers and bikers. They're working on one of their DC–3s that crashed on approach the week before.

The plane, inbound from Soldotna, a little over an hour east, just ran out of fuel in bad weather. The pilot had 300 feet of altitude when the engines quit, and in the frightening silence, he aimed for a road to his left. At 100 feet, he saw he wasn't going to make the road and braced for a landing on the soft tundra. The wheels tore through the mossy ground cover right down to the ever-solid permafrost, and the plane slammed to a halt in just 150 feet, nosing over like a bird with its feet nailed to a board.

The trip over on the nose was a long split second, according to the pilot, because he thought the plane was probably going to tumble end over end for a while, probably killing the hell out of him. Miraculously, it settled back on its tail wheel, and Winky was able to tow it out of the ruts in the tundra with his surplus army truck. He towed it by the tail, back onto the road, and over to the airport, where the pilot and everybody Winky can spare is trying to get her flying again. The pilot walks around his plane with an energetic spring in his step and smiles easily, having shed some primal tension by walking away from that crash.

He explains, "I wake up every day and feel like I've gotten away with something." In the winter, he flies the DC–3 in the Bahamas. "You want to touch me?" he asks, just as my 206 pilot strolls over with the word that the skies over Egegik have cleared.

The Grounds

The Egegik River flows north from a deep tundra pool called Becharof Lake and makes its way in loops and swirls for most of its fifty-mile length. The Egegik carries a heavy load of silt and effluvia from the unstable terrain to the south and deposits it into Bristol Bay to form awesome tidal flats that defy imagination. On the high tide, the flats are awash, forming the favored channels for the spawning migrations of red salmon—productive but very risky grounds for drift gillnetters. The flats at Egegik, like those at the mouths of the other great rivers of the Bay, are perfect, though, for setnetters.

These fishermen set up camps along the bluffs, set their gillnets out below the high-water line, and let the wind and tide carry the salmon to them. On the ebb, they pick the nets and either fly their own fish to King Salmon or sell them to a buyer on the beach who consolidates the catches of several setnetters and flies bigger loads to Anchorage or fish plants on the Kenai.

Reaching Egegik, we land on a crude cargo strip in front of the International Seafoods of Alaska (ISA) beach plant, which is owned, lock, stock, and barrel, by the Reverend Sun Myung Moon and his Unification Church. The place was known as Hermie's until ISA bought it in 1982 during the church's colonial push into the Alaska seafood industry. (They also built a bottomfish plant in Kodiak.) New, tidy red-and-white buildings form a compound inland, back from the berm where the beach ends and the tundra begins. Highlighting the scene is a big sign facing the Bay: $2.10, the sign says, apparently the price they're paying for red salmon that day.

As I move my pack and tent off the runway, I watch a pair of forklifts hauling fish totes from the biggest of the ISA buildings to a staging area on the beach. In the painter's light of late afternoon, the yellows and silvers of the forklifts are snappy against the flat, gray-brown tones of the sand. In that light, the colors are so purely sensual that they edge over into the same realm as the sounds of the beach, the uneven snarling of the forklifts, the clatter of equipment against the cement floor in the building, and the distant whine of a Honda Big Red, one of those three-wheeled, all-terrain vehicles that now infest Alaska.

At odd moments, the more insistent sounds fade and give way to a kind of basso background hum that seems to come from every direction. I search for its source, finally looking offshore, where, for the first time, I see the fleet: hundreds of boats barely visible but shimmering in the rippling mirage between the sea and the sky beyond the mud flats, three miles away. As the picture of the place solidifies in my senses, it is shattered by an asynchronous murmur that grows quickly into a sound I know as heavy aircraft engines, big radials of the old sort turning high rpm.

And then it appears, maybe fifty feet off the deck, left wing down in a bank around the contour of the point where I am standing, its gear and flaps up, speed maybe 200 miles per hour, buzzing the beach to clear it for a landing. The roar builds to earsplitting but exhilarating proportions. Though I have hung around airports all my life, I have never seen a four-engine transport at high speed so close to the ground. Usually, when they're that low, they're in landing configuration, with gear and flaps down, flying slowly in preparation for returning to Earth.

The plane flashes past, no more than 100 feet from me, and I see the pilot nod as he sees me. "That's really something, isn't it?" says a man's voice behind me, as the noise level drops and the plane banks away over the sea for its approach to land. I turn to see an unlikely, shortish guy in wools and boots with a camera dangling from his neck and a red ISA baseball hat over a pair of bookish eyeglasses.

"Did you hear about the other one?" the guy asks, shifting his stance to face down the beach in the direction of the river. Perhaps because of the hazy afternoon light and shadows, I have failed to notice it until just now, a gray smudge against the bluff about a half-mile away. No, from this distance it looks like ordinary beach junk, and my eyes would not have lingered.

"Did you see it?" I ask the visitor.

"Oh, yeah," he says. "What are you doing here?"

At this point, I fall into what I can only describe as Moonie paranoia. Maybe it's that particular question put so bluntly; maybe it's the camera and the feeling I've been photographed without knowing it; maybe it's simple intolerance. My past experiences with the Unification Church have been positive, though I have had to temper my opinion of people who trade their responsibility for the major choices in their lives to remain blissfully childlike in the care and control of Rev. Moon.

And then there is the matter of Rev. Moon himself and his very real connections with Korean arms dealers and his perception of himself as the savior of the world—not *one* of the saviors, but *the* savior incarnate—and the fact that Father, as his followers call him, just this week has gotten out of a federal slammer on the East Coast after doing a little time on a tax rap. Most of all, though, I suppose it's the fear I can't suppress that arises from one of the tenets of their faith that permits any action or deception if it furthers the Rev.'s goals for his church and his side action. They call it "divine deception," and it was explained to me by some pleasant church members in Kodiak a few years earlier when they were getting their bottomfish plant going there.

The people of Kodiak just about went berserk in 1979 when ISA bought the waterfront site and built the plant; it was one of only two in Kodiak at the time that could process bottomfish. There were anti-Moonie marches in the streets, outrageous harangues at city council meetings, and ugly threats. But ISA stayed and migrated to the Bay the next year. The church also owns fish plants and fleets on both the Gulf of Mexico and the Atlantic. "We're into food. It's just that simple," I was told in Kodiak by Joe Spiciani, the son of a New York brassiere manufacturer, who joined the church and became a fish plant manager. "We need businesses so our members can work and raise families, and what's better than food?"

"But why do you remain children all your lives?" I asked him. That was a long time ago in Kodiak. He was slated to be married soon in one of those mass weddings for which Rev. Moon is famous, but which have less than a 50 percent success rate.

"Who doesn't?" Joe answered.

People who have competed with ISA get a little hot about free labor and church subsidies and the like, but most who sell fish to the Moonies—many Egegik Beach setnetters, for instance—have few complaints. "They pay the highest price, they sell us food and fuel without gouging us, and they're good neighbors," says one woman whose family has been fishing at Egegik for several generations. "I think they're a little odd, and I wouldn't want to be one of them, but nobody's asking me to. And besides, this is Bristol Bay, and not much of anything out here is exactly what you'd call normal."

An Eyewitness

Divine deception or not, I decide to talk to this guy on Egegik Beach. He is the first person I've run into who knows what happened for sure. I ask him if there were survivors, but his answer is lost in the roar of the arriving DC–6, which has now returned to land, kicking up tons of sand as its props howl in reverse thrust. "Everybody made it," he repeats. "There were three in the crew. It happened at night. We got there right away and pulled out the bottom of the cockpit with our tractor from up on the bluff. The guy you really want to talk to is down there, though." He points toward the wreckage. "He was in his cabin on the bluff when it hit. Let's go. I'll ride down there with you."

He walks back to the ISA camp and immediately returns with a Big Red. On the way, he shouts his version of the story over the noise of the engine. The plane was carrying 30,000 pounds of salmon, a normal load for a DC–6, and was bound for Kenai. It was owned by Ball Brothers, a Dillingham company with a lot of experience on the Bay, and flown by a crew of three—pilot, co-pilot, and flight engineer. Darkness had fallen when the pilot attempted the take-off, and he apparently was unable to pick out a reference point in the blackness ahead to tell him he was drifting left on the beach, into the bluff. Just before pushing his throttles to take-off power, the pilot is reported to have said, "God, it's dark down that beach." And just as he rotated the nose gear to leave the ground, the entire, screaming mass of aluminum, steel, fuel, and fish started to come apart.

When it hit the bluff, the aviation gas fueled a fire so hot that the aluminum of the airframe melted into puddles on the beach. The flames were visible for thirty miles across the dark, hazy Bay, competing for brightness with the late-rising full moon that might have lulled the pilot into thinking he could make the night take-off. The salmon saved the crew, as it turned out, by piling up between the cockpit section and the wing roots, where the fire was most intense. And the weight of those fifteen tons of salmon moving forward when the plane stopped split the cockpit away from the flames.

People from camps along the beach arrived almost immediately, led by the ISA LARC, a big steel amphibious vehicle with a powerful winch. The rescuers maneuvered the LARC onto the bluff above the cockpit, and some unnamed hero skidded down the bank into the flames to throw the cable around the twisted metal. From inside, a terrified voice shouted over and over, "I've got men down here! I've got men down here! Help me, Help me!" Just that. And they were beating on the side of the plane.

The salmon started burning, too, the fleshy scent mixing with the sour odors of rubber, metal, and gasoline in flames. From the LARC on the bluff, the rescue crew took a strain on the winch cable, bringing anguished cries from the cockpit. The cable was wrapped around someone's leg, so down into the flames went the rescuers, this time with a chain saw that had materialized from someone's camp. Then one man was out, then another, and finally all were safe on the bluff.

Dr. Demi and the Angel

Even a week after the crash, the wreckage is terrifying, a reminder of transience and uncertainty of the highest order. We are just not accustomed to viewing an airplane of that size on its back, spindly landing gear pointing up, with shredded tires reaching for the sky. An airplane upright, poised to travel through the air, is a permanent truth, and images do not exist to prepare us for its opposite condition. Had the carnage been total, the sight might have been easier to bear, but as it is, the familiar shapes of the plane remain to remind me of what it once had been.

One huge engine is buried in the gravel of the bluff, driven into the primal till by the enormous force of impact. And the fish are everywhere, charred and discolored by the inferno and spread in a stinking glacier flowing from a big crack in the fuselage just behind the cockpit. My guide from ISA leaves me. He says he has to go to work.

I continue to prowl the alien scene, touching nothing and glad no one has died here, for then I would be guilty of gross irreverence. I walk up onto the bluff to look down on the plane. Miraculously, the setnetter's cabin, situated right over the wreck, is untouched. As I look it over, a man comes out and stands by my side. I notice the shadow of a wing burned into the tundra at my feet. We say nothing, exchange no greeting for maybe a minute, until I break the silence and say, "Hello."

"I was in the cabin, right here. I thought it was an angel's wing," the man says, glaring intently at me in a kind of stagy way. He looks a little like the actor Keenan Wynn. I ask him if he is, and he says no, he's Dr. John Demi, a newly retired chiropractor from Paradise, California, and he had never even been on a plane until he came to Alaska that year to visit a friend who owns the setnet site. His voice cracks with an anxious tension that I suspect has been there since the crash.

"We were asleep, in there," he says. "I heard the plane taking off, but that happens all the time, and I didn't think anything of it. Then it got real quiet until the crash and fire right outside the window, where the wing landed. I said, 'The hell with this,' and started running that way." He points across the tundra. "I thought the cabin was going to explode.

"I think I got about a half a mile and came back when I remembered that those guys in the plane needed help. We got them out," he says, smiling as though he's discovered a delight that has been missing from his life until then. "Have a drink," he says, passing me a bottle of cognac I hadn't noticed. Then he says, "I want to show you something." I take the cognac, and he disappears into the cabin.

Dr. Demi returns and edges around to stand between me and the bluff, forming a faintly lit silhouette in the evening light. Behind him are the lights of the fleet, just winking on, and the shimmering presence of the wrecked DC–6. He is cradling a twisted piece of aluminum, clearly molten once but now cooled in the shape of a running dog. It's a good three feet long.

"A greyhound, right?" says Dr. Demi, starting to laugh heartily. "I've got another one inside that looks just like a jockey. Can you believe it? I got to say this is one of the oddest places on Earth, but now I'll come back until I die.

"I really thought it was an angel's wing, come to take me to heaven, you know," and he hands me the greyhound. "Here. You want to hold this?"

The beach at Egegik is still a kind of garden spot for Bristol Bay setnetters, though the air show isn't what it was. International Seafoods of America still buys fish and has kept its reputation as a good neighbor, and the tides continue to bring salmon and hours of backbreaking labor for the fishermen. I tried to find Dr. Demi, but no luck.

A Beautiful Place to Be

SALMON TROLLING ▪ SOUTHEAST ALASKA, 1987

"Most trollers have a lifetime deal with their gear and the fish.
It's very personal and they don't usually want to talk to anybody about it.
When the fish are feeding, you can throw anything down.
When they're not, that's when the clever gear guys do better."

—Jon Rowley, ex-troller

On harbor days in the 1920s, Alaska salmon trollers pounded spoons, hunkering in their boats in the timbered lees that became Port Alexander, Point Baker, and Port Walter in the Alexander Archipelago we usually call Southeast Alaska. They snipped rough shapes from sheets of brass and copper, placed the metal over hollows carved in ironbark blocks, and, with small ball-peen hammers, tapped out subtle curves and shapes until hunch or experience told them to stop. The lures the old trollers hammered were crude in that manner of handmade things, each one different from the one before. Nonetheless, they were variations on a theme that later would produce the Superior, Kachmor, and MacMahon king salmon spoons.

During lulls in the storms that drove the trollers to shelter, the *tink, tink, tink* of hammers hung in the air with the pleasant aromas of the north-coast rain forest. The bucolic pleasures and rewards of the most independent of all Alaskan fisheries brought many trollers back season after season for their entire lives. Take Toivo Anderson, a Finn, who ended up in Southeast after a Bering Sea ice storm drove his prospector father's immigrant family from its first settlement in Nome, 2,000 miles to the north. Toivo was seventeen years old when he took to the trolling grounds in 1927, fishing first from the F/V *Flower* with cotton lines, bait, hammered spoons, and the genetic savvy of a bred mariner.

He fished his way into the F/V *Yakima III*, which he bought from Fred Wooleson, the "Yakima Kid," a troller only slightly less of a legend than Toivo himself would become. In 1947, Toivo built his first boat from the keel up, the F/V *Greta*, and three years later, he and a few of his running buddies pioneered the Fairweather Grounds, a pair of sea mounts that lie between twenty-five and fifty miles off the coast south of Yakutat. The towering mass of Mount Fairweather dominates the vista to the east of the grounds.

Toivo and the few other trollers who learned how to fish the Fairweather racked up unbelievable scores for many years, until dams, people, and management tangles took their toll in the 1970s and cut fishing time everywhere. His best day on the Fairweather, he remembers, was 282 large king salmon, "sometime in the late sixties." (A good day for a troller under most circumstances is 50 kings.) Toivo and his pals passed their locations and information on hot lures and bait over the radio in a coded language that sounded like a Norwegian record played backward, according to one eavesdropper who tried desperately to learn their ways. (The language was Finnish, of course.)

"Trolling was a ball in those days," Toivo says. "Oh, I don't know why I did okay. I was lucky. I've always felt that this was my life, and I just tended to my business and kept my gear in good shape. When I was young I was a little gung-ho, I guess, and I changed gear a lot. I tried a lot of stuff and just found out what worked and changed it when it didn't. I did all kinds of stuff; I painted spoons myself when we figured that out for cohos. Chartreuse is a great color," he tells me, "or those yellow Canadians. Hootchies? Oh, I like the Golden Bait 111 [four-color, mostly greenish] or 39 [turquoise] or 71 [yellowish-green]." He laughs, knowing that I know he is either telling me his secrets or shining me on. "And I've used hotspot flashers and some Abe and Als, but I never mix them."

Toivo lives in Sitka now and says he fishes "easy" with his wife on their latest and last boat, F/V *Sea Haven*, a big, comfortable offshore troller. "I guess I don't know anything different," he says. "It was a real free life, and if you have a little bit of initiative, you can do okay. Everything depends on your own initiative and what you pick to catch the fish. I like that."

Rigging Gear for Trolling

What you use to catch the fish. The subtleties and complexities of catching big salmon with hooks and lines are reflected in the gear, and many trollers confess to nothing short of obsession with their lures, lines, and boats. They use three basic types of lures. Painted or unpainted spoons come in a variety of shapes and lengths and flutter as they are trolled. Wood and plastic plugs are virtually all of one shape, conical with a wide-notched mouth tapering steadily to a pointed tail. Generally measuring three to seven inches, they swim rapidly from side to side. Hootchies (which get their name from hootchie-kootchie skirts) are made of soft plastic and look rather like miniature octopi, cuttlefish, or squid. Unweighted, they are often rigged on the leader behind thin, flat, chrome-finish flashers, which aren't unlike large (usually twelve-inch or more), hookless spoons. The flasher serves as an attractant and gives the attached hootchies a darting action that salmon like to see in their next meal. Fishermen also use whole or cut herring, capelin, or candlefish, sometimes behind a flasher, sometimes not. Some trollers soak their bait in brine to toughen it up; some don't. Bait is a pain in the neck, but usually outfishes lures.

When he starts fishing, the salmon troller first lowers his boat's two long wooden or metal poles so that they extend from each side of the boat. Serving essentially the same function as the short outriggers of an offshore sports fisherman, these trolling poles vary in length, but forty-footers are about right for a forty-foot boat. Securely attached to each pole at even intervals are three heavy, vertically hung "tag lines." (Trollers are limited to four lines in most places, but they once fished as many as eight or ten with a complex setup of lines and fair-leads.)

Stiff springs are rigged between each tag line and its pole, with a small, tinny bell on each spring. At the lower end of each tag line is a bronze or stainless-steel device called a "clothespin." The tag lines and their clothespins serve as the attachment point for the gear that actually does the fishing, a set of main lines made of $5/64$ or $1/16$ stainless-steel trolling wire. Each wire is marked by hand or at the factory with pairs of brass beads clamped at intervals of two to four fathoms, depending on the fisherman and the kind of salmon he is after. The wire is spooled onto the reels of hydraulic power gurdies, really small winches, which are mounted in series on the rails on each side of the boat. As each trolling wire is set, its free end is first run from the gurdy through a hanging block, or fair-lead, that swings from a davit of galvanized pipe extending over the side of the boat.

Next, the wire is passed through the clothespin of a tag line and attached to a large, lead cannonball. Trollers use fifty-pounders for the main lines and thirty-five-pounders for the bag lines trailing aft so that the latter will run shallower and not foul the mains. Each cannonball is attached to its line with a leather strap; if the cannonball hangs up on the bottom, the strap will break before the wire does, or at least that's the idea.

After the cannonball is lowered over the side, with the strain being taken by the gurdy, the troller begins to attach his spreads, each consisting of a length of monofilament leader, maybe a flasher, and a lure or bait. At each desired interval on the trolling wire, the troller uses a longline snap to attach the spread, sometimes including an eighteen-inch piece of quarter-inch rubber called a "snubber," which absorbs the shocks of a fighting salmon.

As he snaps each spread to the wire, the troller lowers it farther into the water until he reaches the next attachment point, and so on, until all spreads—from four to twenty or more depending on the depth and location of the salmon—are in the water. When all the spreads are on the wire and the cannonball has reached the desired depth, the troller snaps on a plastic "stopper" just inboard of the tag line clothespin through which the wire has been running as the spreads were attached. This device stops the further passage of the wire through the clothespin. Now, when the troller reverses the gurdy and allows the tag line to swing away from the boat, the stopper comes up hard against the clothespin and effectively maintains the depth of the fishing wire as it moves out to its trailing position off the pole.

There are, of course, variations in the procedure used to set troll gear, and it's only complicated when you try to use words to describe it. Once a troller gains a little experience, he can set four full lines of gear in ten minutes or less.

A Beautiful Place to Be

> *"When that spring starts pumping at the end of a trolling pole,*
> *it's just as exciting to me as it was the very first day.*
> *And it's always a beautiful place to be."*
>
> —Jerry Schrader, psychiatrist and ex-troller

Catching salmon with hooks continues to seduce commercial trollers on the Pacific grounds from California to Alaska. A hard worker can still make a living at it, even though the fish no longer show up in the hordes that once left even the most jaded fisherman breathless. Most trollers admit, though, that making a living by tricking great game fish into biting hooks has an allure beyond making a living. They describe their work in terms of common sense, mystery, enthusiasm, and art, and always with caveats of humility. Ask a troller, whether a legendary highliner or a novice, what kind of spoon, hootchie, plug, or technique works best, and he'll almost surely begin his answer with "Well, I don't really know too much about it," or another statement to that effect.

What a troller does know about goes something like this: It's morning on the Fairweather Grounds or on the Prairie off Washington's Olympic Peninsula, or Fish Rocks off the Point Reyes bluffs, or any of thousands of other places Pacific trollers set their gear into the sea in an act of faith typical of few occupations. The boat is small by ocean standards, say forty feet. Like the majority of trollers, she's made of wood, with a six-cylinder diesel under the house, and with berths below, under the foredeck. Her hold space aft is binned for ice, though many trollers have blast freezers these days.

The run this morning through the darkness in a gentle, westerly swell is just another one of those wheelhouse interludes with a cup of coffee and a cigarette, followed by a resolution to quit, then breakfast off the oil stove, which also nudges the chill out the sliding door and onto the deck. Eating, the troller watches his LORAN ticking its way toward yesterday morning's numbers, where he had a flurry of action, a clatter, and fifteen large kings before 8:00 a.m.

The troller stands up, grabs a handful of Coffee Nips—a kind of hard candy his girlfriend turned him on to—reaches under his worn-out captain's chair, and throws the handle that shunts hydraulic fluid through hoses to the gurdies. He engages the autopilot and then leaves the house. The deck is slightly awash, the ocean soughing through the scuppers with the roll of the boat. The troller surveys the sea at first light, seeing shearwaters and white-belly petrels, which are good signs. His senses quicken as he takes his place in the chain that begins with the sun and links phytoplankton, percolating like ginger ale off the bottom; zooplankton; invertebrate scavengers; needlefish and herring; salmon; and finally trollers.

There, in the stern, are his lures, carefully lined up on the deck shelf behind the trolling pit. (With few exceptions, trollers are compulsively neat about their gear.) The baits—herring, because nothing beats it in the early spring—were prepared the night before. They're clipped into E-Z baiters with single hooks and stowed just forward of the trolling pit in a ten-gallon trash can like the one in which *Sesame Street's* Oscar the Grouch lives. The troller's daughter gave it to him for good luck, and it has lasted three seasons already.

From the rack over the trolling pit, he takes his morning spoons, two of the old, heavy Superiors that he won in a pinochle game from Radio Eddie, whose father had them for thirty years before that. He never uses them when he knows there are sharks around or inshore near rock piles. They go on the bottom of his main wire on long, six-fathom, 100-pound test monfilament leaders, and he believes in them.

For the rest of the spreads on his mains, he'll use bait, since he'll have to work that gear a lot more often than the flashers and hootchies he'll put on the lines that run behind the boat to Styrofoam floats, called pigs or bags, and then down. For the bottom of each of the bag lines, he picks a plastic plug, white with a green strip for mornings.

As the troller sets the last of his lines, the sun breaks, fracturing the surface of the sea along the wind rifts and the rippled wake of the boat, moving at two knots or so. Trollers run slowly for kings, and faster for coho later in the summer. In the pit, the troller checks his depth sounder, disengages his autopilot by a remote control, and adjusts his course. He pops a Coffee Nip into his mouth and settles his hips on the back of the pit, noticing for the first time how chilly and damp his oilskins feel this morning.

He talks to himself—"Okay, we're fishing. Yes. Good morning"—
and he looks over his deck back to the house to see that everything is
neat and set up as he likes it, with no one to please but himself.

He chants, "Come on, salmon, bite the hook." He heard a sport
guide do that once when he was a kid, just before he felt the astonishing power of a king salmon almost tear the fishing rod from his young
hands. He looks around at the birds; they're hitting the water more
now, right where he is. "Yes. Come on, salmon . . ."

There. On the starboard main, the inside tag line on the pole.
There. *Tink. Tink, tink, tink. Tinktinktinktink.* And then the whole pole is
shaking, and the spring is stretched way back, and he can feel the bulwark and cap rail shudder under his fingers. He checks the sounder to
make sure he isn't on the bottom. No. It's okay. Then there goes the
bell on the port bag line, as the troller reaches to engage the starboard
main gurdy and bring in the main line.

The salmon on that main is a hog, a big hog. The troller can see
the wire slash the surface of the water as the fish lifts the line, cannonball and all. The wire comes to the boat, allowing the tag line to
slacken. The troller opens the clothespin, freeing the wire and feeling
it directly for the first time. The fish is still there, and now the port bag
is taking another hit. Then more. "Yes," the troller says, aloud.

The spreads come up on the starboard main wire, which is really
jerking now. The troller takes off each spread as it comes up, coils it,
and places it carefully and tangle-free on the deck behind the pit. Each
clip is snapped, in order, to a piece of wire on the bulwark. He removes
one, two, three, four, five spreads; now there's only the spoon left in
the water, and that is where the big fish must be. "Yes," he says again.
The biggest fish are on the bottom a lot of the time, the real monsters.

And then there it is, like a shiny, fifty-five-gallon drum. The troller
has taken hundreds of big salmon over thirty pounds, but this one has
him cranked up a little. The salmon is on the long leader, easily cruising at faster than boat speed, moving abeam. The brass flash of the
spoon is clearly visible at its head, and then the fish senses the boat and

dives. The rubber snubber between the leader and the wire stretches from a foot and a half to about four feet, quivering. The fish is well hooked. "Sharp hooks. Always sharpen hooks," he thinks, not even knowing now if he spoke aloud, his mind now wholly with the salmon.

The troller leaves the spread clipped to the main wire and reverses the gurdy, lowering the wire to soak the still green fish, to let it fight itself out against the cannonball and the snubber and the boat. Agonizing minutes pass, no doubt for the salmon, too, when the hook can tear from the bony mouth of the fish or simply break. The troller brings the spread up again. This time, when he pulls against the salmon with his hands, the fish moves. No longer is it like pulling a line that's eye-bolted to a wall. The troller gains a couple of fathoms. The fish runs, out and down, and then under the boat. Damn. No. Then he's back alongside, just ten feet out and right abeam, cruising. He still looks strong. The troller feels a cold pain as the mono opens up an old cut in his hand. More soaking time. Then back up.

And now the salmon is bleeding and he comes easier, rolling on his side to flash white and gold in the beautiful morning light that seems to be a part of the fish instead of reflected from it. The troller makes an anxious survey of the water near the boat, hoping not to see sharks or sea lions, either of which would gladly fight him for this fish. He finds nothing threatening. The salmon is alongside now, and the troller can smell it, actually smell it. King salmon have a smell unlike that of any other kind of creature, a deep, musty odor suggesting moss and earth, of all things. The troller reaches down familiarly for his gaff, hanging in the pit.

Easy. Easy now. He reaches down as far as he can toward the salmon and, with a practiced touch, raises its head slightly out of the water, snapping the heavy end of the gaff down on a spot about an inch back of the big eyes, killing the fish instantly. With another snap of his wrist and forearm, the troller sticks the metal point of the gaff into the fish's head and hoists it aboard and into the checker bin ahead of the pit. He has to use both arms.

The fish will go sixty pounds, maybe seventy. Its head and back are deep black, dissolving like shades of lacquer from ebony through a brightening spectrum of dense tones to the silver of its huge flanks. The troller reaches into the bin and slaps the meaty side of the fish, smiling, barely realizing he has done it. Then he turns the salmon, takes his spoon from its jaw, and gets to work on the other lines. The salmon, if it dresses out at fifty-five or sixty pounds, will be worth more than $100, the morning maybe a million.

Tools of the Trade

Catching salmon with hooks and lines is a symphony of fishing gear, and choosing spoons, hootchies, plugs, and rigging absolutely consumes most trollers. Some change gear constantly and buy everything they can get their hands on. Others settle on a half-dozen different hootchies and a few coho spoons, use some bait in the spring, and let it go at that. Mike Moore and Einar Ask have been selling gear to trollers for a decade at Seattle Marine and Fishing Supply. Einar, himself a troller, is also the son of a well-known pioneer troller, Ingvald Ask.

Though trolling gear is not a big-ticket item like trawls or seines, Mike, Einar, and the others in the gear trade court the trollers with catalogs, color charts, and bargain prices offered through trollers' groups and co-ops. People who sell trolling gear seem to tend the mystique with a mixture of knowledge, amusement, and almost childlike enthusiasm for the vast selections of hootchies, hooks, plugs, and spoons. A troller can buy "off the shelf," or, if he's willing to order six dozen or more of whatever he wants, manufacturers such as Silver Horde, Golden Bait, Luhr-Jensen, and Gold Star will custom-make his gear.

"What's hot in terminal gear changes from year to year," says Mike Moore. "Some stuff is standard, and a lot of people use it. Some guys seem to buy more than others, some buy what catches their eye, and some know exactly what they want when they walk through the door."

The Science of Sense

A hootchie or spoon that catches a fisherman's eye won't necessarily catch a fish's eye, though that obvious statement has more profound implications than are readily apparent. "The root of our problem in selecting fishing lures is our tendency to think of fish in terms of our own sensory perceptions and to equate their detector systems with our own," says Paul C. Johnson, author of the classic book *The Scientific Angler*. Johnson has worked for twenty years as a fishing gear designer and researcher for Berkley & Co. of Spirit Lake, Iowa. Most of his work has focused on freshwater game fish, but many of his observations apply to both freshwater and saltwater fishing.

"Ask the average person which of his senses is the most important and he will generally choose vision," Johnson says. "But if you could pose that same question to a game fish like salmon, the answer would be his intricate, marvelously sophisticated vibration-detection system. Deprive a fish of his sense of vision and he can and often must survive quite handily. Not so if his vibration-detection system has been altered, though. In his aquatic world, the loss of this sense spells certain death."

The vibration detectors, or mechano-receptors, in fish are cells, typically found along the lateral line, that respond to vibrations or low-frequency underwater sounds. Used in harmony with the fish's other senses, this sensory system explains why lure action is so critical to commercial fishermen. Without a doubt, the most enchanting set of signals a fish can receive is one emitted by an easy meal. Presenting a salmon with a natural or artificial lure that appears to be a crippled bait fish is the name of the game. Period. The action of a lure will trigger a strike with mechano-sensory, visual, and electrical stimuli. The mechano-sensory system, however, probably delivers the most important information to the brain of a fish.

In his book, Johnson reports on the work of Dr. Fred Janzow, an ichthyologist who probed the ability of fish to survive in the extremely low visibility of cloudy or deep water. Janzow used bass for his experiments, designing small, translucent, plastic eye cups that he attached to the eyes of the bass so that they could not perceive anything but ambient light. They must have looked pretty silly, but the eye-cupped bass had no trouble locating minnows, which they attacked directly, apparently with no need to chase around looking for them.

Ichthyologists continue to report major findings that generally confirm what commercial fishermen have learned over the years by trial and error. For instance, use the lightest leaders possible because the salmon really can see them. Heavy leaders also kill lure action and present a "too disturbed" or "less disturbed" prey target to the fish. When choosing leader material, use clear monofilament because it's the most invisible. When the sky or sea is dark or cloudy, select fluorescent lures because of their greater brightness underwater.

Salmon Eyes, Salmon Nose

The visible electromagnetic spectrum—in other words, color—is an orderly energy arrangement described in terms of wavelength, or nanometers. The spectrum of visible light runs from violet (380 nm) through shades of blue, green, yellow, and orange to deep red (750 nm). Shorter (ultraviolet) or longer (infrared and radio) waves are invisible to the human eye and, generally, to a fish underwater as well. At the surface, though, fish may be able to detect the ends of the spectrum that are invisible to humans.

The practical conclusion from this cursory study of the spectrum explains why chartreuse comes up so frequently on the "favorite color" list of commercial salmon trollers. Chartreuse, lying between green and yellow, is at the precise middle of the visible spectrum. Moving away from chartreuse in either direction on the color chart means moving toward the less easily seen. At trolling depths, chartreuse is simply more visible than other colors, and we even paint our fire trucks chartreuse for that reason.

In addition to their work on color and vibration, Johnson and others have proven that some "smell tracks" repel fish, some are neutral, and some attract fish. Many commercial trollers have learned the same lessons from experience, but an equal number appear to have approached the matter of smell tracks and discarded it as inconsequential to their success at catching salmon. Biologists, though, have established that a fish can detect concentrations of chemicals or compounds in amounts as small as .0000000017. That's the equivalent of one drop of chemical in an Olympic-sized swimming pool, or one drop of vermouth in 300,000 barrels of gin. A fish's sense of smell is much more acute than that of a dog.

"I talked to everybody I could about smell, and everybody had a different perspective on it," says former troller Terry Johnson. "I think some guys are compulsive and do a lot of work cleaning gear and such, convincing themselves it's doing some good."

And listen to Toivo Anderson: "Washing gear? That has been shot down the tubes." But then he adds, "Just keep it clean. I used detergent and kept oil off it."

Then there's this from Troller X (who asked to remain nameless): "A friend of mine who worked as a fish counter at McNary Dam [in Washington] told me he'd rub a stone with his hands and throw it in where the fish were milling around and they'd stay away from it. But if he picked up a stone with a glove on and threw it in, they'd come to it. I don't know. I don't really wash my gear or my hands in any special way. I'll put a piece of herring under a hootchie for smell, though."

Says troller Frank Caldwell, "There are guys who just cannot handle troll gear because of the way they smell. I heard once that nobody but a Finlander smelled just right," he says, laughing at his own exaggeration. "I shampoo my gear with Joy [detergent] in a bucket of warm water. Drip oil on a gurdy wire and it'll kill you."

And so it goes.

Tricking Salmon

Any troller in his right mind would welcome and use any research or advice that made his occupation more of a science and less of a guessing game. Still, when you get right down to it, the uncertainty of trial and intermittent reward is an important element in the appeal of trolling, as is the endless variety of choices. Clearly, however, some gear works better than others.

Many trollers use bait during certain parts of the season, particularly in the spring, while others use none at all. Among the traditional choices are herring, needlefish, and, off California, anchovies. Making generalizations about troller preferences is risky, however, because trends change. One example of such a shift is under way off Northern California [in 1987], where trollers have long used bait almost exclusively but are now going more to artificials.

The main types of terminal gear other than bait used for salmon trolling are hootchies, plugs, unpainted metal spoons, and painted metal spoons, and variations on these basic themes.

Captain Yamashita and His Hootchies

The Japanese-made plastic artificials got their name from their resemblance to the "hootchie-kootchie" skirt made famous in vaudeville and the movie *South Pacific*. Although the name is pure Americana, a man named Kusutaro Yamashita invented this lure in Japan in 1941. The captain of a tuna boat, Yamashita was shipwrecked during a storm, and while he was in the water, he observed that fish were biting at colored rags and bits of cloth floating in the wreckage. Surprised, he reasoned that if fish would respond to such material, he might use artificials instead of bait. Or so the story goes.

Captain Yamashita was rescued, of course, and later started the Yamashita Fishing Tackle Co. Ltd. He asked the plastics industry to provide him with a material that would be soft enough to resemble a fish, but be strong, thin, elastic, and durable in freshwater or salt water.

Once perfected, the hootchie came to North America through Nikka Industries of Vancouver, British Columbia.

Hootchies for salmon trolling are made in six body types, namely, in descending order of size, Octopus, Cuttlefish, Plankton, Miniplankton, Needlefish, and Anchovy. Each size is made in up to 300 different one-, two-, three-, and four-color patterns, some with glow-in-the-dark pigments. Upward of 5,000 combinations are possible, and many trollers create even more varieties by leaving their hootchies in the sun to fade, or painting them, or pulling out some of the tentacles, or fishing them two at a time, one over the other.

The Japanese hootchies distributed by Luhr-Jensen carry the Sound Wave brand name. The manufacturer claims that molded bumps and ridges on the surface of the plastic cause the gyrating hootchie to emit an attractive sound. As usual, some fishermen swear they work, and some dismiss them as folly.

Troller X, who in 1986 caught 5,800 cohos and 600 king salmon in Alaskan waters, lists (by brand and color number) the following hootchies as his biggest producers: Sound Wave 36C (main color chartreuse); Sound Wave 29C (blue); Golden Bait 35 (grayish green); Golden Bait 104 ("The Birthday Party," four colors: green, blue, pink, and white); Golden Bait 2 ("The Fourth of July," red); and Golden Bait 39 (turquoise). The highly successful hootchies are used by so many trollers they take on nicknames, such as "The Birthday Party," that become part of the vernacular. Troller X never uses whole bait, but often wires a small piece of herring under his hootchie, a time-consuming process that involves fine copper wire that's wrapped around the hook eye and run down through the bait strip. Troller X is famous for trying just about anything to catch salmon, and one year, though he laughs about it now, he painted the bottom of his boat with herring-size streaks of silver paint to attract fish. "Every one of them grew a beard in about two weeks," he says.

Thirty-five-year veteran Frank Caldwell, owner/skipper of the F/V *Donna C* and author of the fine book *Pacific Troller*, says his favorites are the four-color hootchies. "I walked into a gear store a few years ago and saw the new multicolor jobs," Caldwell says. "I thought, 'That's a hootchie that'll catch fish,' and they did."

Decoys of the Deep

Plugs were once carved painstakingly from wooden blanks, like duck decoys, and were real works of art. But today their plastic counterparts are nowhere near as popular as they were twenty-five years ago because of the success of hootchies. Nonetheless, they're still in common use. Washington coast trollers seem to use more plugs than Alaskans, according to gear dealers Moore and Ask, among others. The biggest manufacturer of plugs is Tomic Lures of Canada, but a wide selection is also available from Silver Horde/Gold Star and other makers. Except for Martin Tackle's Spar-X plugs, which are turned from Alaska cedar, all modern plugs are of hand-painted plastic. The solid-color plugs are made of ABS, a compound noted for its hardness. Glow-in-the-dark plugs are made of Butyrate.

Because of the handwork and savvy required, many troll gear makers are small, often family-style operations, and most got their start when plugs, not hootchies, were boss. Silver Horde, for instance, was started by Lew Morrison in 1948 and is now owned by Barry Morrison, his nephew. "Lew used to farm mink, and at one point they had a bad year," recalls Barry in his Lynnwood, Washington, workshop. "With the last bit of money they had, the family bought a plug mold and turned out one of the first plastic plugs. Lew worked with Rex Fields, who was the first with the plastic plug."

Now Silver Horde makes eleven sizes of plugs, from three inches to seven inches long, in no fewer than 400 color patterns. Barry's son, Kelly, who is twenty-three, does all the painting, taking on a few assistants during the busy season. Manufacturing a product with so many variations isn't easy, but the demand is there. "We listen to the fishermen. They talk to us," says Barry. Silver Horde has also acquired the Golden Bait and Gold Star lines and has urged the Japanese firm that makes hootchies under these names to use color patterns similar to those in plugs of the same brand, and vice versa.

Generally, trollers prefer dark plugs in clear water and light plugs in cloudy water. Plugs are usually fished without a flasher, but the combination is not unheard of. "One time, I helped a guy fix his gurdy shaft and saved him a fifteen-hour run to town," says Frank Caldwell. "He wanted to do something for me and told me he was dragging a particular kind of plug behind a flasher and catching kings in this one spot. I know he wasn't lying to me, but I tried the exact same setup and couldn't catch a one."

Spoons of Mystery

The large, unpainted spoons usually used only for king salmon are the descendants of the earliest artificial trolling lures. They have evolved into fine-tuned, durable representations of bait fish and see a lot of use. Varying in length from two inches (a No. 2½ spoon) to six inches (No. 8), they are punched in dies from brass, copper, or a combination, then either left unfinished or chromed over all or part of their surfaces.

The Superior, MacMahon, and L.G. Johnsons are old designs owned by Luhr-Jensen. Silver Horde/Gold Star also makes king spoons, as do several other American and Canadian companies. The highly respected Kachmor comes from Martin. One Canadian king spoon, the P–28, has been especially popular with Alaskan trollers for decades. The older Superiors are among the heaviest spoons available, and some trollers claim their weight makes them fish better. Chrome/brass combinations are reputed to have the edge in clear water, while copper/brass combinations get the nod in cloudy water.

Painted spoons catch a king or two once in a while, but generally are known to trollers as coho gear. "When it was coho time, I just put on the little red spoons," says Jerry Schrader, a psychiatrist-turned-troller who then went back to shrinking heads. He describes himself as having been a midrange producer on the grounds. "I had $5,000 worth of other coho spoons, but I could have just thrown them away and used red," he says. Some of Schrader's running partners say psychiatry is perfect training for trolling.

Dr. Schrader's red spoons notwithstanding, most trollers agree that you can get pretty bizarre with coho spoons, the most often altered, painted, bent, and otherwise adjusted pieces of gear in a troller's inventory. Gear makers also get more orders for special coho spoons than for any other kind of gear.

"A guy will come in here and grab a chartreuse black dot Johnson No. 5 and say, 'Can you put the dots on like this?'" says Kathy Evans, store manager at Seattle Marine. Holding the spoon in question, she continues, "This one is a Luhr-Jensen, and they'll do what he wants on special order. Then the guy's buddies will call, and then others want them, and pretty soon it's a stock item." Still, almost every troller will tell you he's painted his own coho spoons at least once.

The basic shapes for coho spoons are the Manistee, a pointed teardrop (by Luhr-Jensen) that comes in sizes from two inches (No. 2) to three-and-three-quarter inches (No. 5); the Canadian, an elongated oval (by Silver Horde, Luhr-Jensen, Gold Star, and others) in sizes from two-and-three-eighths inches (No. 3) to five-and-a-quarter inches (No. 6½); the LuPac or MorPac, a stubby oval in two-and-a-quarter inches (No. 1) and two-and-three-quarter inches (No. 2); and the similar Luhr Pac.

By their action, some coho spoons represent crippled prey, and others mimic startled, healthy, fast-moving prey. The smaller coho spoons imitate the motion and vibrations of schooling bait fish, on which coho are likely to feed more aggressively and less selectively than king salmon. A red dot, representing the eye or gills of a startled herring or other bait fish, is a proven attraction, according to both fishermen and scientists.

The variations in coho spoons are myriad, as are their paint schemes, which may involve single colors or combinations, including white, pearl, purple, blue, green, chartreuse, flame orange, orange, golden yellow, red, and cerise. Troller X says his favorites are as follows: for the glacier waters west of Cape Spencer, he likes the chartreuse Canadian, which he modifies by adding dots of Revlon flame-red nail polish; in clear water, he likes the LuPac in flame red; and he's also partial to the No. 4 Manistee, colloquially known as "The Chip," in chartreuse/fire dot and cerise/black dot. Toivo Anderson says he likes the lemon-yellow Canadian, anything chartreuse, and the 50/50 chartreuse and turquoise LuPac.

All spoons have an up side and a down side, and the hook has to be attached with the tip up, since the center of gravity is in the shank and curve. You want the hook to ride through the water with the tip up. The common hook for coho spoons is the Mustad 9510 No. 5 or No. 6. Larger hooks should be used for faster boat speeds, which many fishermen feel are a must for cohos. "I don't think you can troll too fast for cohos," says Troller X.

Though most trollers settle on a standard repertoire of a few spoons, plugs, hootchies, flashers, and hooks, the temptation to try new ones or go back to old ones is hard to overcome. "Fishermen want what's new," says gear dealer Mike Moore, as he handles a plug he says is the ugliest he's ever seen. It's a six-inch Tomic 145 colored deep yellow with three orange stripes. It's called, by some, "The Peanut Butter" plug.

"This gear thing can become kind of an obsession," he goes on. "Say you and I are equally skilled fishermen, and something new comes along on the market. If you see it first, you're going to be forced to give it a look, at least a look. If you don't, I might, and if it works, I'd have an edge on you. Last year, for instance, we saw better fishing through chemistry," Moore says, holding up an inch-long Cyalume lightstick that will glow for eight hours after activation. "It killed some of the purists to come in here and buy these things, and the jury is still out on them. I know of some guys, though, who have been using them religiously and just killing the fish." The light, apparently, attracts salmon at depth.

"Once I bought some hootchies as a joke," says Jerry Schrader. "They were a mix of pink and orange and green, and I gave them to a guy I knew and told him, 'These are really going to do you.' Then one day Arnie, that's his name, calls me on the radio and says, 'You know those crazy hootchies you gave me were catching king salmon all day yesterday.' So I put some on and I caught seventeen fish right away. Whatever works is what works.

"The hallmark of a troller," Schrader continues, "is patience and consistency. You can't really predict the time of day the fish will bite or which hootchie will produce, so the idea is to put in a consistent day, day after day. The more hours you put in, the more fish you put in the boat. It's a pretty good game."

—⁓—

Salmon trolling is no longer the good game it once was. The Fairweather Grounds, once open year-round to king salmon fishing, are open for only a week or ten days now. The fish that make their way past the legendary sea mounts are mostly of Canadian or Washington origin, and treaties restrict the catch off Alaska to a fraction of what it once was. Then, too, the whole idea of going way out to sea, away from the spawning streams, to catch salmon is falling out of favor because near-stream fisheries are much easier to control. In the 1990s, a lot of trollers are also longlining for halibut and black cod, or spending a good part of the year working another job. To have gotten in on wide-open trolling was an enormous stroke of luck.

Fishing with Modest Ambition

CODFISH TRAWLING ▪ KODIAK, 1987

Along the wrinkled hillside above the Kodiak waterfront, Gary Neilsen drives his pickup through the darkness of an Arctic night in February, with his girlfriend, Shirley, there on the seat beside him, cowboy-close. Inside the truck, over the noise of the heater fan, Gary and Shirley are talking about the weather, or an errand that has to be run while he is out fishing, or any number of intimate matters that are like secret codes for couples of long standing. Gary Neilsen, twenty-nine, is the adopted son of the son of a fisherman, and he is the skipper of the eighty-nine-foot trawler *Royal Baron*. He has been delivering cod, pollock, and flatfish to a plant in town, making trips of four days to a week, depending on the weather. In February, it can range from bad to terrifying. Shirley Malutin works in the office at one of the fourteen seafood plants that crowd the Kodiak shoreline for about a mile.

When Gary's father, Mickey Serwold, turned the *Royal Baron* over to him three seasons ago, he told his son, "You better catch fish." Just that. As the family story goes—and they have a videotape to back it up—Gary cruised back into town on one of his first trips with a deckload of fish and a full cod end in tow. "It was outrageous," Gary says now, telling the story again, the delight still bringing the high tones of excitement to his voice. "Delivering in town sure beats the hell out of joint ventures," he adds. "It's gotten a whole lot better with markets just in the past year. Lots of plants in town are doing bottomfish."

Island Terrific in the North Pacific

This wild island where Gary and Shirley live was once an outpost of Russian fur traders—the *promyshlenniki*—and later became a whaling and sealing port of substantial magnitude. Like a geologic tourist colliding with the continent, Kodiak crouches along the volcanic coast of the Alaska Peninsula where the shallows of the Gulf merge with the beginnings of the Aleutian Trench. Though treacherous in its natural vagaries, the region has been a fertile producer for humans for all of our history. Aboriginal Aleut villages remain on some of the island's bays; the city of Kodiak itself has a population of about 7,000, mostly Caucasians and Asians.

The Kodiak city site, on Chiniak Bay at the northeast end of the island, can best be described as a going concern, with streets, sidewalks, and things to do. When Alaska crude from the North Slope oil fields fattened the public purse, a share went to Kodiak for harbors, a bridge to Near Island, schools, roads, and other community projects. On the night Gary, Shirley, and I are driving to the boat, for instance, a basketball tournament and a play about poet Emily Dickinson draw hundreds of people to the high school, a facility so modern and innovative it would be the centerpiece of any American city. But even before the oil, Kodiak prospered from its connection to the abundance of the surrounding sea.

With all its apparent civility, Kodiak remains an enigmatic combination of easy living, the hardships of a remote outpost, and invigorating challenges. Its character vacillates between that of a religious enclave and a day-care center for adults; its people are given to extremes and hardened opinions. Wilderness pragmatism and the heroism of independent living are part of every transaction. In Kodiak, one of the motels will rent you a room for $52 unless you're willing to sleep over the bar, in which case the price is $38. It's your choice.

Just about everybody in town has cable television and a VCR, and the network programming is from Detroit via satellite, on Eastern Standard Time. The bars—Tony's, the Mecca, Ships, the Village, Shelikof Lodge, Breakers, and Solly's Office—are mostly windowless caverns with an emphasis on forgetting and remembering that leads not infrequently to all the usual gestures of comfort and irresponsibility. In Solly's Office, so named because its three phone booths are the only office a lot of fishermen ever have, you'll find the most indestructible men's room short of a prison cell. The urinals are a pair of stainless-steel troughs; the stall is an enclosure of quarter-inch hull-plate steel that is tack-welded to two-inch-pipe stanchions and bolted to the concave concrete floor, which has a drain in the middle. The men's room is clean, but every surface shows signs of having withstood unsuccessful assault; the graffiti ranges from literary allusion to frightening derangement.

Like most of the bars, Solly's has a restaurant on the premises. A friendly waitress named Joan seems to know when you need just a cup of coffee and lets you feel okay for not ordering a full meal. If you ask, she'll tell you that she and her carpenter-husband moved from Alabama to Kodiak "for the money." Her voice carries no hint of apology regarding motivation.

Besides Emily Dickinson and cheerful basketball festivals, Kodiak has a college, aerobics classes, a well-heeled senior citizens' center, an orchestra and chorus, pizza, politics, and arguably the most spectacular scenery and outdoor life in the world.

The island was devastated by an earthquake in 1964, when it actually tilted through a six-foot arc and a tsunami smacked the shore, throwing boats hundreds of feet up the surrounding hills, among other things. The green and buff hills that soar into mountains around the island were tucked and folded by the doomsday quake, and today they look like the loose skin of one of those Chinese shar-pei dogs. But Kodiak is healthy now, recovered from the quake, and with the prospects of a full-fledged, year-round bottomfish processing industry starting to shimmer, even better days could be ahead.

The fishing pattern in Kodiak has generally been salmon in the summer and "something else in the winter," as one waterfront character put it. In the past, that "something else" has been shrimp, then king and tanner crab. At the beginning of the eighties, it became apparent that shrimp and crab had done cyclical disappearing acts and that the foreign bottomfish fleets were on borrowed time. American fishermen wanted them out of the U.S. zone. In response, the state sunk some money into a bottomfish demonstration plant in Kodiak. And down the beach, the Reverend Sun Myung Moon's Unification Church built International Seafoods of Alaska, a modern plant for the cod, pollock, and flatfish that glistened as the future for the faithful and the world.

Unfortunately, though, despite other tentative forays into shoreside processing, none of the fishermen or packers who sniffed bottomfish in the wind were able to take the wisp of promise to the bank. So for six years after the initial attempts to kick off the bottomfish boom, until just now, the "something else in the winter" was pessimism and irritation, especially because the joint-venture trawlers delivering to foreign ships at sea were getting rich. It was a tall order to get them to abandon the easy money to pioneer shore processing.

The *Royal Baron*

Kodiak's harbor is protected from all but the vagrant southwesterly wind, which happens to be howling now as Gary hangs a left down the hill to the waterfront. The demarcation between the sea and the land is a collection of intermittent lights, glowing in clusters around the plants and in lines on the fingers of the floats on the dock. The night air is clear, and as the pickup dips down onto the flats along the water, the wind loosens its grip in the lee.

The *Royal Baron* is ready for sea, tied up at the International Seafoods dock outside the *Green Hope*, a company trawler that is being unloaded by a shrieking, high-powered fish pump. Gary and Shirley sit in the truck in the muddy plant parking lot talking, oblivious to the noise. Out the windshield, they can see a herd of about forty sea lions lolling at the gurry outlet from the plant, rolling over each other in a lazy feeding waltz, barking from the backs of their throats, which flash pink in the dock lights.

The *Royal Baron* began life as the U.S. Army TP–99 tug *Sgt. James A. Burzo*, built in 1944 at the Clyde Wood yard in Stockton, California. She was launched into the embrace of the San Joaquin River with a quick and efficient ceremony typical of the war years, when thousands of ships and boats were built. Measuring eighty-nine feet by twenty-five feet by twelve feet, she carries the heavy timbers, planking, and decks typical of her era and class. Originally, she was fitted with a 450-horsepower Fairbanks-Morse diesel, a gargantuan piece of machinery by modern engine standards. Horsepower now comes in more compact packages.

Foss Launch and Tug bought the *Sgt. Burzo* in June 1950 for $7,678 at a government auction. In keeping with tradition, Foss renamed her after a family member, Margaret Foss, the eldest daughter of Drew and Donna Foss. The tug was then stationed in Southeast Alaska, serving the fuel run there until 1962. By then, her engineers had had enough of the old Fairbanks-Morse, so Foss laid her up for repowering. Circumstances intervened, however, and the new engine was never installed. The *Margaret* was retired and put into dead storage in Tacoma, Washington, until January 1966.

That winter, she went back to sea to begin her fishing career under the hand of Olaf Angell, a Seattle fisherman. Angell removed the Fairbanks-Morse, which actually protruded above deck level, and installed a more powerful but smaller 500-horsepower Caterpillar C379 that is still her main power. He renamed her the *Baron* and put the boat to work in the nascent North Pacific king crab fishery, which would become the greatest fishermen's boom in history.

In 1977, Mickey Serwold bought her and added "Royal" to her name, giving her a job on the Alaskan shrimp grounds. Crab or no crab, Mickey was (and is) a trawler, and that's what he was determined to do. Until the oceanic warming trend and other factors decimated shrimp stocks in the Gulf of Alaska, the fishery was a steady payday for the Kodiak winter fleet. King crab stretched until the winter of 1982 before breaking; then most Kodiak fishermen just protected themselves as best they could while biology chiseled deep gouges in the island's economy.

Serwold kept the spacious and stable *Royal Baron* at work as a research charter and tow boat. She dragged off Kodiak for a short-lived Portuguese salt cod joint venture in 1982 and for a Taiwanese joint venture in 1983. In 1984, Serwold turned the wheelhouse of the *Royal Baron* over to his son, Gary, whom he had adopted when he and Patti, Gary's mother, were married in 1970, just before moving to Alaska. Now, with Gary on the bridge and boat payments ancient history, the *Royal Baron* is set up just right for a few good paydays in the emerging shore-based bottomfish business.

The Smell of Money

As the old saying goes, the stink of fish is the smell of money. Aside from the usual fisherman's business of surviving at sea and catching fish, the puzzle that presents itself to the shore-based bottomfish trawler and processor is, of course, economic. The departure of foreign catcher boats from the Bering Sea and Gulf of Alaska essentially released about 2.5 million tons of what are generally referred to as bottomfish—cod, pollock, flatfish, and rockfish—to American interests.

Ten years after passage of the law that banished foreign fishing fleets from U.S. waters, two-thirds of that amount was being taken by about 160 fishing boats in joint ventures with foreign processing ships operating offshore. In February 1987, the price for pollock delivered at sea (after no handling at all aboard the American catcher boats) was $130 per metric ton (2,200 pounds). Crew shares for five-month stints on a U.S. joint-venture boat soared as high as $100,000 or more.

The second element in the equation that is driving the American fleet in the U.S. zone is the growing fleet of U.S. factory trawlers and processing ships. The third element, and the one most crucial to Kodiak, is the shore-based processing industry. It's a tough nut to crack because the big money is in joint ventures, and it's hard to pay off a big loan delivering fish to the beach, so most trawlers would rather deliver offshore. Still, about a dozen boats were off-loading at plants in Kodiak, and equipment to process the fish was steadily flowing into town. Seven of the fourteen plants in Kodiak were actually buying bottomfish during the winter of 1986–87. The price of pollock delivered to shore was $.08 per pound, or $176 per metric ton, compared with about $.06 per pound offshore. Unbled cod was bringing $.19 on shore, bled cod a penny or two more per pound. Flatfish, including sole and flounder, were worth about the same as pollock. All prices to the fishermen were going up, though, as competition for deliveries increased.

"It's great to see what's happening in Kodiak," Gary Neilsen will say later. "It's one of those rare moments among fishermen when the little guy is perfectly positioned to make some real money. The *Royal Baron* is the right size; it doesn't cost much to own her. If you have a low-overhead operation, a paid-for boat will help . . . and modest ambition."

Modest ambition. Gary was in high school during the king crab glory years in the late seventies and early eighties. Eventually, he left his childhood position as a deckhand on a shrimp trawler, opting instead for the big time. "A lot of us were making more money than our high school teachers," he says. "Some of us kept fishing; some went to college; some did all kinds of things. I was young and dumb," he says, with the kind of humility in his face usually seen in much older men. "I had a new truck, a motorcycle, a great apartment, and the best-looking girl on the island.

"Taxes?" Gary's verbal question mark is clear. "I never thought about anything like taxes, but the Internal Revenue Service did. And I'll tell you, I fished my way out of that hole, thousands and thousands of dollars' worth, in joint ventures for months without a break. I like the way I fish now. I like coming home."

"Every fisherman in this town tried not to go joint-venturing," says another fisherman, Dave Harville, who owns four trawlers, a longliner, and, in California, a troller. "I just can't afford to bring one of my trawlers here to deliver to a shore plant. You can't take a boat worth $1 million and bring it to a $500,000 market." Harville thinks the dramatic expansion of the American offshore factory trawler fleet will precipitate the biggest change in the balance between joint-venture and shore deliveries. "When our efficient factory trawler operations get going," he says, "the shore plants won't be able to absorb all the refugee boats displaced from foreign joint ventures. There just won't be enough fish to go around." (Under the Magnuson Act, boats fishing for American offshore and shore processors have priority over joint ventures in the allocation formula.)

But Harville, among others, is already sounding the overcapitalization alarm. "King crab was never this bad," he says. "We are wildly overcapitalizing in trawling, mainly by building too many expensive factory trawlers. If you look around the world, you'll see a lot of factory trawlers tied to the docks; then look at the Americans rushing headlong into factory trawlers. Small to medium trawlers will stay in business. All-American joint ventures with U.S. processing ships and U.S. catcher boats will work, too. In five years, you're either going to be in a very successful business or you're going to be out starving," Harville continues.

"In eighteen months [from February 1987] you'd better be where you want to be with your debt service structured right. You're not going to be able to take a $600,000 boat and make $1.5 million a year like you can now in joint ventures," Harville warned. "The cash is here. Now. You have three choices: get in, make every dime you can, and bail out; get in, fortify, and modernize for quieter times; or just take the money and spend it, don't prepare for the future, and go broke."

The major competition for the Kodiak shore plants—and those in Dutch Harbor 1,000 miles west on the Aleutian Chain—are the off-shore catcher/processors, also known as factory trawlers, which are both fishing ship and factory. The fishing capacity of the fleet is already approaching the maximum sustainable yield set by the management council, with no differentiation between quotas for offshore and on-shore deliveries. Dutch Harbor, behind the leadership of its mayor, Paul Fuhs, himself a former cannery workers' union organizer, is pushing for a local priority zone in which only American boats and shore plants would be allowed to process bottomfish.

Kodiak fishermen, though, have generally been outspoken opponents of that kind of exclusionary regulation, which they view as a threat to their independence and free enterprise. "I'll fight priority access as long and as hard as I can," Dave Harville says, "but that's the answer for this town. That and full multispecies processing so that you can sell a shore plant everything you catch, not just cod and pollock."

Harville's opposition to a protective zone around Kodiak is shared by Oscar Dyson, one of the elder statesmen of Alaskan fishing and part owner of All-Alaskan Seafoods, which has both on-shore and off-shore processors. A member of the North Pacific Fishery Management Council, Dyson has fished off Kodiak for forty years and pioneered the king crab fishery. "I don't favor a zone to guarantee supplies for Kodiak processing lines," he says. "I ask the question, 'How do you get the most fish to the most people for the least money?' That's what this business is really all about."

Outbound

Gary kisses Shirley and swings down out of his truck. He walks past the yammering sea lions and climbs down the twenty-foot face of the dock onto the *Green Hope*, where the plant crew is halfway through the unloading. The overhead dock lights bring sharp contrasts to the scene, losing the dark shapes in shadow and flashing bright on the silver tube of the fish pump, the white hard-hats of the crew, and the bellies of the codfish in the hold. Five minutes later, Gary has awakened his crew, who spent the night aboard the *Royal Baron*, and settled onto his bridge for the ride out of town.

A steady routine takes hold aboard the *Royal Baron* in winter. She leaves Kodiak for the grounds with her holds iced and runs from three hours to a day or more. If the weather is fishable, she drags the submarine bluffs and edges around the island for Pacific cod, the money fish, as well as pollock and flatfish. Each tow can produce from nothing to 30,000 pounds or more. She will make up to four tows in a day, with her skipper and crew of three working from first light to dusk. When her hold is full, or the groceries run out, or she breaks down or loses a net or gets beat too badly by the sea, the *Royal Baron* and her crew go home. The routine flirts with monotony, but the images that fill the hours and days at sea do not.

Consider, for instance, bucking the weather with no load, outbound at dawn, the bow tracing sickening, hyperbolic arcs. The boat's descent is punctuated by sheets of spray that rattle on the wheelhouse in a relentless, chattering attack. Inside, remaining dry seems odd and temporary, despite the hints that assure safety: warmth; the unmistakable aroma of onions frying in butter drifting up the ladder from the galley; the reassuring clicks and squawks from the electronic panoply on the bridge; and the easy morning-voice of the skipper.

"It's almost fishable. If I didn't have to tow into it I'd give it a shot," Gary says to me. I'm braced against the bulkhead that runs across the pilothouse, a landsman pathetically seasick, aboard to learn, firsthand, what the days bring to a trawler delivering North Pacific bottomfish to a shore plant in Kodiak. Minutes pass. "It's not fishable. The radio says it'll get worse before it gets better," Gary pronounces, passing the word to his crew. "We'll anchor in Ugak Bay and wait it out." Already, the anemometer on the after bulkhead of the wheelhouse is tickling forty-five knots, signaling a widow-maker howling out of the southwest.

The wheelwatch is passed to the junior crewman, Richie Heglan, a man making his first trip on a trawler after many years at sea on the crab grounds. Two months earlier, he had to leave his berth on a crabber in Dutch Harbor because his teeth were hurting him so badly he couldn't work. Now he's had them all pulled and is fitted with plates. He's marking time and trying to make a little money before going out west to the Bering Sea again.

The rest of the crew consists of Kit Anderson, the deck boss, and journeyman Gary McCormick. Anderson is a fortyish dark Norwegian from another Pacific fishing town, Astoria, Oregon. He has been a fisherman, a seal hunter, and, for what he now knows was too long a time, a Green Beret in Vietnam. McCormick is an Aleut, a descendant of one of the thousands of family bands that were once nourished by the abundance of the North Pacific coastal zone. Their numbers were eventually decimated by Russian fur traders who also include the city of Kodiak in their legacy.

As Gary and the crew not on watch sleep en route to the anchorage, I remain in the wheelhouse to keep the horizon in sight and breakfast, eaten earlier, under control. The pounding continues, at times sending a vicious shudder through the trawler. The wind tears at Kodiak Island and the surrounding sea for thirty-six hours. During the layover in Ugak Bay, the crew sleeps, plays cribbage, eats Kit's cooking, and watches videotapes of network television shows recorded for them by Patti Serwold, Gary's mother. On every tape, there's an episode of *Amerika*, a hideous piece of anti-Russian propaganda; on Ugak Bay, the tension and conflict that fuel nationalistic madness on television are absurd.

Beachcombing brings relief. Even in the bone-chilling cold, the seductions of exploration are irresistible, so the crew goes ashore in shifts. Steep talus slopes form the shoreline of the twenty-five-mile-long fjord, with mountains rising to 4,000 feet, their peaks invisible in the leaden winter sky. The rocky beaches are littered with bright-orange buoy balls from lost crab gear, and slightly inland, the huts of salmon setnetters lie dormant in their winter plumage of temporary disrepair. From the beach, the *Royal Baron* is a green-and-white island against the spectacular backdrop, and it's not hard, looking over it all, to get the feeling that you're getting away with something out there. "I grew up here, in this amazing place," Gary says.

Going Fishing

On the morning of the third day, the wind slackens, and Gary fires up the Cat and takes the *Royal Baron* to work. "All I got to do is find the edge," he tells me on his bridge, as the trawler dances in the trough of the settling southwesterly. "None of this matters," he says, sweeping his arm in an arc to include the electronic array around him, "unless I see this." Gary walks to an ancient paper depth recorder and flicks his finger against the carbon-black smudges that represent balls of cod from the previous trip. It's an old Simrad paper machine, one that Gary says has been on the boat since 1966. To find the edge and the fish, he also relies on a Simrad CS112 color sounder, a Si-tex Honda HE32 paper recorder, and, for inshore work such as research charters, a Wesmar SS165 scanning sonar. He has a pair of Furuno radars, an FR1800 twenty-four-mile and an FR3600 thirty-six-mile; Simrad LC204 and Furuno LC70 Lorans; and a now-indispensable Furuno G102 video plotter. His communications hardware includes two CBs, two VHFs, a Hull single sideband, an AM radio, and a ghetto blaster for tunes.

"I don't care if you tell everybody what I use to catch fish," he says. "Everything I have is an antique, so they can't buy it anyway. When the fish are here, it's not that complicated." Perhaps not to Gary, but he's been a fisherman all his life, nourished in an adolescence that most young men only dream about, earning tens of thousands of dollars from high school on. And he's fished a full joint-venture season on the Bering Sea, so he has a fair idea of how to catch fish.

And he does this day, in three tows on the sixty-fathom edge outside Ugak Bay. The groaning old Rowe Machinery deck winches accompany the work like the background tones of a Sibelius symphony. They're cold, hollow noises that suit the icy deck and the black water over the side. The *Royal Baron* packs about 80,000 pounds, with about 60 percent codfish that are bled and iced; the rest is pollock and flatfish not worth the trouble of bleeding. For the Alaska shore-based dragger, cod is king, commanding three times the price of pollock, though pollock and the many flatfish are becoming more and more worthwhile. When someone figures out how to efficiently tender the low-value species from the grounds to shore, eliminating the long runs by catcher boats, these fish might bring better paydays.

In these tows, halibut, salmon, and other species prohibited to trawlers are few in number, and they are culled quickly from the catch and put overboard, some still alive. As for the rest of the catch, the bleeding operation is a backbreaking chore performed in a crouch, hour after long hour. The enthusiasm of the green crewman fades quickly; he will never, as it turns out, make another trip as a trawler.

Each tow is about two hours long, and since the fish settle to the bottom only during daylight hours, fishing ends with sunset. The weather looks good, and the routine is set: a run into an anchorage just inside Ugak Bay, out on the grounds to begin fishing an hour after sunrise, and back to the anchorage. In winter, the fish are there, and the weather holds; so four days later, the *Royal Baron* runs to town in a following southwesterly.

Coming Home

The simplicity of trawling is found at sea; ashore, the complexities of economics and politics shatter the *pax marinas*. Gary Neilsen and the handful of trawlers grinding out a living around Kodiak are competing for a piece of the North Pacific bottomfish boom with the factory trawlers just now coming on line in force. Soon the competition will intensify, and the economic realities of getting the most food to the most people for the least money seem to argue against shore-based operations.

The cost of paying fishermen to spend a day or longer hauling fish back from the grounds is almost prohibitive in the lean economics of bottomfishing. Even now, only boats with very low overhead can hack it. Some kind of efficient bottomfish tendering scheme is a gleam in every shore-plant owner's eye, for he would no longer have to pay a fishing machine to haul the catch to town. Full vertical integration of fishing fleet and processing plant could be another key to success. A plant such as International Seafoods, which owns its own catcher boats, is in a much better position to ride with the markets.

"We're doing okay for now," Gary says. At the first harbor buoy, Gary calls Shirley on the marine radio to find out where she parked his truck. On the air, their voices reveal relief, affection, and the security of routine. Two days after the *Royal Baron's* lines hit the dock at the plant, the boat will be ready for sea again. The crew will change, because turnover is high when a share from a single trip doesn't buy a sports car. By the end of April, though, Gary will have tallied the highest scores in history for a shore-based trawler delivering to Kodiak. He's twenty-nine years old and thinks he has a future as a fisherman.

Gary Neilsen is still running the Royal Baron,
he and Shirley are no longer a couple, and thanks to the
political muscle of the Alaska congressional delegation,

delivering bottomfish to shore plants is routine. Under pressure from the politicians who were promoting jobs for Alaskans, the bottomfish allocations were split into on-shore and offshore quotas, ensuring that the offshore fleets wouldn't take it all in competition with the slower-paced on-shore plants.

Fishing the Flats

SALMON GILLNETTING ▪ PRINCE WILLIAM SOUND, 1987

The background music on the Copper River Flats is jazz on this early morning in early May, a lament from Stephane Grappelli's plaintive violin through the tinny wheelhouse speakers aboard the gillnetter *Christine Sue*. The rhythm competes with the racket of a gale, a sixty-knot screamer driving rain and spray over the boats in the meager shelter behind a hummock known to fishermen as Egg Island. Max McCarty and Noel Pallas have set their net, and after the customary few minutes out on deck looking for the splashes of snared salmon, withdraw to the relative comfort of the cabin. They will let the net soak for a couple of hours as the endless dawn of the Arctic night turns into its slightly grayer cousin, the day.

Visibility is a quarter-mile or so; you can just barely see farther than the end of the gillnet, which is suspended from a bobbing line of white corks on the surface. The 900-foot monofilament net is strung between a pair of bright orange buoys, fluorescent against the silty brown water of the delta. A good haul for a single set on the Flats is 100 fish; a great set is 400. Legends are made of 700-fish sets that can literally sink a boat. Each fish is worth about $20 at this day's price, an astonishing $2.60 a pound if the fisherman bleeds the salmon, ices it down, and delivers it to the plant in town instead of to a tender on the grounds. With the fisherman getting that price, Copper River reds and kings are selling in supermarkets for $9 to $11 a pound, and on restaurant plates for between $10 and $30 for a six-ounce serving.

The red and king salmon that swarm in the 300,000-acre delta of the Copper River, its rivulets, and tributaries are the Beaujolais Nouveau of the annual spawning migration that gives the coasts of the Pacific Rim their abundant character. They are the first, and many say the best, of the new runs. Their rich color and high oil content quite simply define "salmon" for discriminating chefs, gourmet diners, and backyard barbecuers. And though all salmon have high levels of artery-clearing omega-3 oils, these from the 430-mile-long Copper River have among the highest. The longer the river, the higher the oil content, because the fish need the nourishment to battle upstream to their final ceremonies of death and birth.

In the 1980s, Copper River salmon harmonize with careful handling by fishermen and processors and the miracle of the jet airplane. A diner in a major-league restaurant in Seattle, New York, or Los Angeles, for instance, can savor a meal of fresh Copper River salmon caught just seventy-two hours earlier on the Flats. Max, Noel, and the other gillnetters begin this chain of events. The world contracts to ten feet by twelve feet inside the cabin of the *Christine Sue* as the wheelhouse windows fog from the vapor of a working coffeepot. Gourmet coffee beans are sold now in Cordova, *Christine Sue's* remote Prince William Sound home port, and the rich aroma of Max's blend mingles with the more pedestrian odors of cigarette smoke, diesel fuel, and damp working clothes.

In the after-port corner of the cabin, drying work gloves and hats are clothespinned to twine strung over the stove, and they sway with the roll of the *Christine Sue* as she jogs in the wind-driven chop. Perched behind the steering wheel on a bench he crafted in his workshop, Max reaches forward to the cluttered dashboard under the windshield. In the working rubble typical of all fishing boats—tools, paperbacks, tide books, a copy of *People* magazine, candy bars, knives, a tin of bag balm for sore hands—Max finds an ashtray and stabs out his cigarette.

Shooting a look across the cabin to Noel, who is sitting over his coffee with his elbows on the galley dinette, Max says to Noel, but also to me to kind of kick off the story of this trip, "Gillnetting is the sport of teenagers." They crack up laughing with the high tones of an inside joke. "Yeah," Noel presses on, "it used to be that the last bastion of the liberal-arts major was law school; now it's gillnetting." Everybody laughs.

Cordova

Max and Noel, both of whom have chewed through the better part of four decades, are fishing together this season on the *Christine Sue* because Noel's boat burned and sank last year. Noel works as a bartender in a chain hotel in Leary, Ohio, in the winter and has been fishing out of Cordova in the summers since the early seventies. Max lives in Cordova year-round, something of a rarity among the 3,000 or so fishermen and plant workers who make their own annual migration to Cordova. They come from around the world in a remarkable blend of diverse styles—some rough-hewn in the tradition of European fishing cultures, others turned out with graduate college degrees, Patagonia regalia, and bulletproof optimism.

The town echoes the diversity of its migrants. Situated on the sheltered shore of Orca Inlet, hard against the tidewater edge of the Henry Mountain Range, Cordova is a visual feast. On clear days, the cobalt blue sky seems to draw the mountains even higher from the silver-black sea. It's days like these that have been known to pull life-long commitments from people who later, when the rain beats day after gray day on the quiet town, wonder just what the hell they're doing in Cordova.

Cordova started as a railroad town, connecting the rest of the world with the Kennecott copper mines via steamship at the deep-water port. Originally called Copper City, the town was incorporated as Cordova in 1909. By the time the mines closed in 1938, fishing had taken hold as the region's staple industry and kept Cordova from joining the ranks of ghost towns. About 3,000 people live there year-round, so the salmon seasons just about double the population. Almost everyone comes from someplace else, whether they are now year-round locals or not, and the traditional gathering spots such as the Reluctant Fisherman restaurant, bar, and motel, can seem like a perpetual waiting room.

Originally from the Tri-Cities area of eastern Washington, Max went to Whitman College and then eased through the counterculture days in a farmhouse in Walla Walla. He's married to Heather, a writer, and together they have two daughters, Hannah and Miranda. "I've had as much fun as anybody," Max says, unselfconsciously making a foray into his own history. "I graduated from college with an economics degree; I cooked on a woodstove; I drove a pickup truck with a big engine. And I fish for a living. I'll tell you, it just doesn't get any better than this.

"I had just always wanted to go fishing in Cordova," he says. "I had a friend at Whitman who came up here in the summer, so I came with him and got into seining. I couldn't believe it. I made $9,100 in three weeks in 1976 and bought into the boat as a partner. We had a thirty-two-foot seiner named *Sugar*, a three-man boat."

Most seiners disdain gillnetting altogether, and disputes between the two types of fishermen approach the proportions of religious warfare. Seiners catch salmon in large numbers by pursing them in encircling nets; gillnetters snare them, far fewer at a time, when the fish simply run into their drifting, monofilament nets. Though Max considers himself to be primarily a seiner, he gillnets to help him make his season. He now fishes the same boat he uses for seining because it is big, dry, and comfortable, although not ideal for gillnetting on the Flats. High-speed, extremely shallow-draft, Spartan jet boats and out-drive skiffs—the marine equivalents of fighter aircraft or sports cars—are the best for fishing the Flats. The vagrant tides and shifting sand and mud prompted one fisherman to describe the Copper River Delta as "too thin to plow, too thick to navigate."

"Anyway," Max goes on, "I moved my family here in '78, so when bad years came, I did whatever I had to to keep things going. I worked on the dam at the hatchery over at Port San Juan [the largest salmon hatchery in the world]. I'm not really a natural fisherman or hunter-gatherer; I'm a natural builder. But fishing is the same in that you get paid for how hard you work. That's a fair deal to me." Max's woodworking skill is a matter of distinct pride with him, and, over the years, he has developed a reputation and a following in Cordova and around the West. "People try to live normal lives against the background of the Flats, though, and that's a mistake," he says. "At best, the Flats are schizophrenic."

The Flats

Here, behind Egg Island, drifting while the net soaks, the *Christine Sue* lurches and shudders as a particularly violent blast is delivered by the wind. A roller smacks the hull with a power that suggests it has risen up out of the Pacific Ocean with the sole purpose of finding us. And we are "inside," somewhat protected by Egg Island, one of several barely emergent bars created by the silt and sand washed from the Copper River over centuries. The topography of the Flats was altered dramatically in ten minutes one morning in the spring of 1964, when, during a great earthquake, the floor of the delta rose six feet. The once-familiar channels, passage, bars, and fishing holes simply disappeared, and new ones took their places. Fishermen had to learn to navigate over the treacherous sands all over again to reach the Racetrack, Poulsons, Walhalla, Gus Stevens, Pete Dahl, Softuk, Kokinhenik, and other well-known drifts on the treacherous grounds.

The Copper River, so named because of the massive copper lode that brought the mines to its broad valley, flows from headwaters on the slopes of the 8,000-foot Mentasta Mountains, 430 miles northeast of the delta. From there, the river first carves an uncertain meander through a soggy high plateau and then tails into a narrow glacial flow through the Wrangell–St. Elias Range of the Chugach Mountains. On the seaward slope, the Copper becomes a torrent. Most rivers terminate in an alluvial fan at their mouths, but some, owing to the composition of the land through which they make their final plunge, or to the power generated by a steep grade, fall to the sea in a brutal, scouring rush. So it is with the Copper, and the strong salmon that are as much a part of the watershed as the river's water.

Fishing the Flats is a matter of understanding tidal hydraulics and staying alive. The flood tide brings the fish over the shallows, where they disperse over 300,000 acres. The ebb leaves them stranded and moving in the channels that surround the shallower water, and it is there that the fishermen set their gillnets. The best fishing—and the most danger—is found where the breakers pound the sand bars. Once, when Max was fishing his skiff, he was trapped by a deadly current in the surf. To save himself, he built a fire right on the deck of his boat, hoping another boat would see him and know he was doomed. It worked, and one of his brother fishermen got a line to him.

The Flats have been declared "non-navigable water" by the Coast Guard, which is a way of saying they take no responsibility for marking them with buoys. The depths and locations of the bars change every year, though, so fishermen get together to mark the channels themselves. The markers are poles cut from straight trees and planted on the channel edges, with radar reflectors hung on them to help in the fog. Each spring, a map of the new channel courses is available from the fishermen's union office in town.

Many who fish the Flats have seen luck go terribly bad, and some die in the sea every year, even the careful ones. The day before this May opening, a couple of dozen drivers climbed into their turbine-powered race cars at the Indianapolis 500, statistically a far safer proposition than fishing the Copper River Flats. "When you're fishing the Flats," Max says, "you're either bored to death or scared to death. But business is business."

The Business

Since the *Sugar*, Max has fished and sold the *Scamp, Sonja, Last Chance, Alert, Moonsong*, and *Miss Wendy*. Alaska limits the number of fishermen in every salmon fishery with a system of transferable limited-entry permits. In 1979, Max bought his seine permit, now worth $100,000, and in 1980, he bought his gillnet permit, now worth $60,000. Still, he is not flush, and he borrowed to buy the *Christine Sue* in 1986. A good season of seining, gillnetting, and longlining for halibut can bring $180,000 gross, with a living wage for a family of four as the net; a bad season of slow fishing, breakdowns, and other bad luck brings maybe $40,000, with no money at all left over after expenses.

When Max started fishing, he sold his fish to tenders on the grounds or to plants in town. The salmon packers in Cordova, and everywhere else in Alaska, are the heirs of a tradition that began when square-rigged sailing ships loaded fishermen, processing crews, and cans for the salmon and sailed north. The captain of the ship became the superintendent of the cannery, an undisputed master, and the fishermen worked for him. The company owned everything, and virtually all of the companies were from California or Washington.

Fishermen traditionally employed seines, gillnets, and traps to catch the salmon. At statehood, in 1958, Alaskans outlawed traps to strike a blow for local fleets and secured a toehold in what would become a steady ascent to total parity in their dealings with processors. In 1974, voters passed a controversial limited-entry statute that created the transferable, exclusive permits for salmon fishing. Only a specified number of fishermen have permits, and if they decide not to fish because the price is too low, packers cannot bring in others to take their places.

This is not to say that all processors were thieving tyrants. Most were energetic entrepreneurs who started at the bottom and worked their way into fortunes. Bob Morgan, for instance, came north in 1941, after a football career at Washington State, with the promise of a job unloading fish tenders for $125 a month—more money than he'd ever imagined he could earn. His second season in Cordova, he became a storekeeper for the canner, selling supplies to the fishermen who worked the Flats from outboard skiffs, the 9.8-horsepower Johnson being the favored engine. They used linen gillnets that required constant care to prevent rot and sold their fish "by the each" to the canneries at whatever price the canneries set. Back then, reds brought a quarter a fish; pinks were worth a nickel. Copper River kings, possibly the best salmon in the world, were worthless to the packers set up for the smaller fish, so they went into "home packs" for the fishermen and their families.

"It was pretty basic," Bob says. "You could get into a skiff, a string of gear, and a kicker [outboard] for a total of about $500. Most of the fishermen were from some old country or another—Scandinavians and a lot of Greeks. Some were Alaska Natives. When I was a storekeeper, I was amazed at the Greeks. They were particularly tough, neat guys and good fishermen. They stayed on the grounds and had their food brought out on the tenders. A typical order was for two loaves of bread, two dozen eggs, and three pounds of garlic. They just added fish. Sounds like a good seafood restaurant these days," he says, laughing.

Bob Morgan eventually became a cannery superintendent and, in 1968, with his savings and money borrowed from fishermen, friends, and banks, started the MorPac plant in Cordova. He sold his company to a Japanese seafood corporation in 1982 and is now a major force in the emerging bottomfish trawling industry. When Bob was building his stake on Prince William Sound, six plants were packing salmon in Cordova and another twenty around the Sound in remote bays and inlets. All the salmon were canned. A fresh salmon was a local delicacy, reserved for the anointed who were willing to come north; frozen salmon were unheard of until the late fifties, and for all practical purposes until the late seventies. "It wasn't that canning was second class," Bob says. "It's just that we didn't have any other way to get the fish to market. Before quick freezing and the airplane, you couldn't give Copper River kings away, and they're the best fish in the world."

Independent fishermen, chartered cargo airplanes, Alaska Airlines, and the nagging sense that a lot more money could be made on these spectacular salmon from the Copper River only came together in 1981, when a new dream took shape. Encouraged by solid prices, growing public acceptance of seafood, and abundant runs due to good luck and smart fisheries management, about thirty-five Cordova fishermen got together and formed the Copper River Fishermen's Cooperative. Co-op fishermen deliver within twelve hours to a tender or plant with refrigeration, eliminating what was once the most destructive period in the gillnet-to-table journey of a salmon. Many fishermen also bleed and ice their fish aboard their own boats, further increasing their quality.

"I sent a box of salmon handled this way to a friend," Max tells me in the steamy cabin of the *Christine Sue*, just before picking up his net. "For some reason, he didn't get them, so they sat on his porch for three days and, still, they were delicious. That was with no refrigeration at all. When you keep them on ice, they're perfect."

To the Table

As the morning brightens, the Flats reveal themselves as long shadows running in gray, horizontal layers. The wind and shallow sea seem to be of the same substance as the sands that take the eye as far as it is able to see in the spray and against a monochromatic sky. A tender will arrive on the last tide of the one-day opening, just as the fishing period closes. Max and Noel will remain on the Flats and wait for the next opening of the run. I will accompany two perfect salmon—one red, one king—from the Copper River Flats to Seattle, where I will eat them two nights later as part of the celebration of the new season's arrival.

On deck, Max wears a full-body suit of orange nylon; Noel is in tin pants and a fleece pullover. From the brown water comes the net, which the men wind on a reel with the help of burping hydraulic power as the corks thump over a roller mounted on the stern. The red salmon, weighing about six pounds each, come over easily. The kings, though, some of which weigh thirty to forty pounds, are gentled over the roller. Noel stands by with a gaff to catch those that drop from the net back into the water. The total for the set is not good—about fifty reds and ten kings. We select two fish and tag them with yellow plastic cattle ear clips. That way, I will be able to follow the progress of the salmon from sea to a table at Triples, a Seattle restaurant that features Copper River salmon in May. The process takes just fifty-six hours from the moment the fish are brought aboard the *Christine Sue*, bled on deck, and carefully iced in the hold.

From Inner Poulsons—the name of the particular fishing spot where the fish were caught—to the dock in Cordova is a two-hour run, but we spend four hours aboard the tender waiting for the tide, which has to be just right to get over the sand bars. At the wrong time, they are boiling with breaking surf. "It's the bars where you get killed," Max says. "No pun intended."

At the co-op plant, the load from the *Christine Sue* is gilled, gutted, and packed again in ice; some are flash-frozen for later shipment. Freezing technology has evolved to the point that carefully handled and frozen salmon are every bit the equal of fresh in blind taste tests. One of the selected pair of salmon, the red, is a female, and her eggs are taken to a special room where Japanese workers salt and treat them for sale as *sujiki*, a great delicacy.

The magic of fresh Copper River salmon just hours from the net is irresistible to restaurateurs and their customers, so the co-op and other packers take the time to ship fresh. Both of the perfect fish are packed in ice for the night to await the arrival of an Alaska Airlines jet, a Boeing 737 known, especially at this time of the year, as a Salmon-Thirty-Salmon. The next day, at the airport, I see near the passenger boarding door three brass plaques recognizing the efforts of the airline crews who tend that section of the food chain for these fish. Engraved on each plaque are the year and the amount of Copper River salmon shipped by air: 1984—1,226,658 pounds; 1985— 1,646,091; 1986—1,307,388.

The flight to Seattle takes just four hours, with one stop en route. From the Seattle airport, a seafood forwarder picks up the salmon and delivers it to a circuit of restaurants and supermarket customers. Triples has been buying full-page ads in local papers since the Copper River run began, drawing crowds to honor the salmon. I gather with four companions to eat those Copper River salmon this night in May, each of us in the business in some way or the other and no stranger to fine seafood. Max and Noel's salmon come to us from Triples' kitchen on a black, lacquered platter as a sampler before we select our main course. The six sauces are subtle blends of herbs, butter, lemon, and garlic; the fish is perfectly cooked, moist and flaky.

The background chatter in the bright room gives way occasionally to the swing beat from a band on the deck, and at our table we tell stories about Alaska and salmon and fishermen. The best stories, though, are on our forks, and when the time for a toast comes, I know it will take hours to tell them right.

—···—

Cordova and Prince William Sound became part of the
lexicon of the evening news two years later, when the
Exxon Valdez *made fools of us all on Bligh Reef, just a*
few miles northeast of town. I was on the Sound during
that terrible time, too, riding with fishermen who rushed

first to try to contain the spill and then dealt with its nauseating aftermath for years. Two years after the spill, Cordova was still a demoralized, grim town, the fishermen had missed a couple of seasons, and the co-op had folded—but life goes on.

The Dream Comes True on the Chain

POLLOCK TRAWLING ▪ DUTCH HARBOR, 1988

In 1978, during the heyday of the king crab boom, Dutch Harbor, Alaska, still had "temporary" written all over it. Its name has been spoken by generations of Pacific mariners and adventurers with the same respect given San Francisco, Vladivostok, Yokohama, and Hong Kong. But Dutch is an outpost, a last chance for shelter, a safe haven on the Great Circle route between North America and Asia before ships traveled at forty knots with little fear of the weather. Fur traders have come and gone, a brutal campaign in World War II darkened the place for five years, and the Aleuts, once dominant, are banished to the nether world of cultural assimilation.

Something new was happening in February 1988, though, as the promise of a steady 2 billion pounds of bottomfish a year was maturing with the encouragement of the American government and an infusion of domestic and foreign capital. The piles of military scrap that infest the Aleutians still speak of hello–good-bye occupation by waves of transients, but chances now seem good that the bottomfish dream will leave something more than junk and broken promises behind.

Beneath the treacherous gray murk through which I am descending on a Boeing 737, another international wave of humanity has rolled up on the beach, perhaps to stay. Dutch Harbor is actually the name of an island in Unalaska Bay. The town of Unalaska itself, across an eight-year-old bridge to a bigger island also named Unalaska, is the seat of government for the community. The 2,000 or so energetic locals, most of whom say they live in Dutch because they like it instead of for the money, stress the joys of independence and resourcefulness as the main drawing cards. The city government has a Department of Parks, Recreation, and Culture and a firm knowledge that, as hosts to a food-gathering juggernaut of a bottomfish fleet, the locals are entitled to a solid piece of the action through jobs and taxation.

Three plants on shore and hundreds of fishing boats, floating processors, factory trawlers, and ships in general commerce are working around the Aleutians. The mix includes Americans, Japanese, Koreans, Russians, Germans, and Scandinavians, either as owners, equity partners, bankers, or technicians. The American claim to ownership of the fish in the sea within 200 miles of the coast is established, but the market, which begins with all the wandering people and money in the fleets, plants, and services, is purely international.

For literally thousands of years, Dutch Harbor has been on the migration route of such ancient tribes as the Inuit, the Aleut, and even the Chinese, who, in all likelihood, reached the shores of mainland North America a couple of thousand years ago. At one time, maybe 900 years ago—when Europe was struggling through plague and constant warfare, and the Vikings were landing for the first time in Newfoundland—the chain of islands we now call the Aleutians was among the most populated regions on Earth. The early people of these islands lived essentially like marine mammals, in small, nomadic bands, and they thrived for the same reason the fishing industry has now arrived: the sea is lush with food, lots and lots of food.

The sea still produces billions of pounds of cod, pollock, crab, halibut, black cod, and rockfish, but now, in Dutch, you can also get a Japanese meal or spicy hot Korean bok choy or a cheeseburger or a steak. The seafood fettucine at the Unisea Inn, the town's central hotel, is so good it should be world famous. The town is sprouting houses, hotels, bunkhouses, and restaurants, all of them modest, mostly prefabricated, and shipped north, but adequate for the adventurous migrants. The stores—a half-dozen more than there were just ten years ago—sell everything from blue jeans and foul-weather gear to gold-encrusted jewelry and video cameras, sold for what the market will bear.

At the gift shop in the Unisea Inn, the best sellers are women's watches (bought by men) and extra-large sweatshirts. "The younger guys buy gifts for their mothers before their girlfriends," Phyllis Giemza, the clerk there, tells me. "And that's good. I have two sons, and I'm glad these boys think of their mothers. They're all kinds of guys, too. Norwegians and Japanese and all. The Japanese will stand here for hours looking at everything, every sweatshirt, and then fold them up real neat when they put them back. Almost everybody is nice in here."

The Bars

Things are a little looser and maybe not so nice at the Unisea's bar next door, where men and women who are either chasing promise or celebrating success gather to drink, dance, and play. The Unisea and the Elbow Room, across the bridge, are full of people looking for jobs, and knowledge of an opening is protected like a pocketful of cash. "If you hear about a job, you don't even tell your best friend," one would-be crabber tells me. "A berth on a crabber can be worth $30,000 for four months' work."

A lot of people in Dutch seem to be "between boats," as the saying goes. The search for jobs in Dutch reaches epic proportions because of the money and the sense that nothing separates a man or a woman from the mass of common humanity like success in so high-risk a place. Some people sign aboard crabbers and trawlers for no money at all for the first trip, an old fishing tradition that can deliver a career or bitter disappointment. When a skipper is at the bar, a steady stream of applicants approaches him, all with the same question. "Do you have a full crew?" If a job is available, you may overhear a short conversation, during which time direct and subtle information is exchanged and a job offered or not. "He's young, like the old days," says one skipper, impressed by the applicant who has just walked away. "He thinks he sees the religion in this thing."

In the bars of Dutch Harbor, you can buy everything from three-dollar beer to tee-shirts to narcotics to the occasional hooker who flies in from Anchorage to get in on the action. On Sunday, though, you can't buy a drink because the city voted itself dry for that one day each week, except for two drinks per customer with a meal. The Unisea is fronted by a forty-foot façade of picture windows overlooking the famous harbor. A television set in a dark corner is on day and night, playing movies, the usual network droning, and, this year, the Olympic winter games.

"This is making me believe in nineteen-year-old women again," says one fisherman, watching the Russian figure skaters. Partisanship broke out during the Olympics, like that strange applause on a TV talk show when somebody's home town is mentioned. One table in the Unisea cheered wildly for the Yugoslavian bobsled team, another for the Jamaicans. The long bar, flanked on one end by the door and a couple of pool tables, has been run for the last three years by a woman named Liz, who works her volatile customers with a blend of spunk and threats. "Esmeralda is my name and giving fishermen shit is my game," she says. "The worst thing I ever saw in here? A fight with Samoans in it about a year ago. There was blood all over the place, and nobody could stop it." What's the best thing she's ever seen? "He's out to sea now," she says, grinning broadly and pouring drinks for the early-evening crowd.

The Elbow Room, over on the Unalaska side, is the senior bar in town, serving whatever horde happens to be wandering through the Aleutians at the time. Named the Blue Fox when it opened in 1942 during the war, the place was a haven for many of the 350,000 American and Canadian soldiers who arrived to drive out invading Japanese armies that occupied Kiska and Attu, 600 miles west, after bombing Dutch. Only one of the three beveled-glass mirrors behind the bar has ever been broken, though stories about monumental bar fights in the E-Room are told in ports from Tokyo to Oslo.

Over the center mirror is a painting of a beautiful red-haired woman in the classical reclining nude pose, with a sign below it that reads "IITYWSIYBMAD (If I Tell You Who She Is, You Buy Me A Drink)." Other signs on the back bar say "Happy Haleutics" (Good Fishing), "Free Beer Tomorrow," and "Jackets, $50; T-shirts, $12." Tacked to the doorjamb is a Gary Larson comic, roughly torn from one of the two weekly newspapers that serve Dutch. It shows a dog wrapped in explosives saying to its disheveled owner, "You want to kick me? Go ahead, kick me. Go ahead." The single four-by-six-foot window in the Elbow Room frames the harbor's inner red buoy against the startlingly vertical volcanic slopes that surround Dutch, but the glass lets only the dimmest light fall on the day drinkers. At night, during the dark months, you can sit at that window and watch the boats turn from the harbor marker toward the sea.

The Fishing

And then, of course, there's the fishing. Three days after I arrive to begin my speculation about all these wandering tribes of humanity, I am aboard the *Storm Petrel*, a familiar, eight-year-old, 123-foot Marco trawler of supreme pedigree. At the moment, Lloyd Johannson, the young skipper, is unscrewing the large filler cap on the gear housing of the port-side trawl winch, inside of which something has given way. The deck is slick with hydraulic fluid, and the air is heavy with those petroleum odors that make you not want to light a cigarette. Worse, we were on the fish after half missing them during the day's first tow, and the hydraulic problem looks bad. Fortunately, the trawl is aboard already instead of in the water.

The *Storm Petrel* is owned by a partnership that includes Marco president Peter Schmidt and the Johannson family of Ballard, a district in Seattle. The Johannsons are a branch of the band of Norwegians who came to the Pacific via good and hard years in the fleets out of New Bedford, Massachusetts. Before New Bedford, the Johannsons, Nesses, Aadlands, and others migrated from the island of Karmoy off the southwest coast of Norway. Vikings. I had come across Lloyd in the Alyeska Seafoods plant office, on the phone with his father, John Johannson, the patriarch of this well-known fishing family. After consulting with the senior Johannson, Lloyd graciously invited me to come along on his next two-day trip.

Losing the time it will take to repair the winch, if it can be repaired, will throw the *Storm Petrel* out of synch in the delivery rotation to the Alyeska surimi plant in Dutch. Our two-day trip will become a three-day trip. The plant, in a new building next to what most people remember as Pan Alaska, was built in 1986 in a venture with Taiyo, a major Japanese trading company, and the Brindle family, old salmon hands who own Columbia Ward Seafood and its subsidiaries. Another surimi shore plant is churning out the high-protein fish paste that is a staple in Asian diets and a highly profitable ingredient in seafood analogs such as King Krab Legs, which are finding a new and booming market in the United States.

The surimi is made from Bering Sea pollock, the mainstay of the fleets, comprising about two-thirds of the annual total of a billion pounds of pollock, cod, flatfish, and rockfish. Three trawlers operate in a delivery rotation to keep the lines at Alyeska running around the clock when the fish are up in the rich shallows of the continental shelf, as they are in February and March. The roe in the spawning pollock, another Asian delicacy, makes the one-to-two-foot-long fish even more valuable to the plant, though fishermen are paid no extra for the roe. Now, in February, the shore price for pollock is $.08 a pound; cod, to those fishing it, is worth $.13 a pound.

The *Storm Petrel*, her refitted sister ship *Sea Wolf*, and the slightly smaller *Morning Star* keep the Alyeska lines running with two-to-three-day trips out to the 200-to-300-fathom edge. That's where the fish are now, just a few hours' run out of town. At the plant, the boats are turned around in twelve to twenty-four hours by efficient unloading teams using high-speed Ryan pumps. Orchestrating the delivery rotation is critical to the quality of the surimi and the roe.

The *Storm Petrel* was built to handle the kind of work she is now doing for Alyeska, and she was a pioneer in the shoreside bottomfish dream that began to crystallize in some minds a decade earlier. She came out of the yard under the hand of George Fulton, a flamboyant, adventurous skipper who had fished around the world in places such as Angola and Chile, and had written a book about it, titled *Good Morning, Captain*. His partners in the boat were Marco's Peter Schmidt and Pan Alaska Seafoods, and all the parties involved knew when they christened the *Storm Petrel* in 1980 that they were embarking on a speculative venture at best.

At her launching, when several hundred of us gathered under brightly colored picnic tents on the West Wall at Seattle's Fishermen's Terminal to wish her well, the *Storm Petrel* was an anomaly. The crab boom was peaking, and joint ventures were cranking up their money machine as the wave of the near future. The Magnuson Act was just four years old, and Japanese and Korean fleets still held sway in the U.S. zone off Alaska.

The *Storm Petrel*

In the late 1970s, the state of Alaska, sniffing the wind for the future, declared its intention to encourage bottomfish processing plants on shore and backed it up with money from the recent oil boom to promote the seafood dream. Unless we develop a profitable system for delivering and processing on shore, the Alaskans reasoned, the fleets of the new era will come from Washington and Oregon, and the promises of the Magnuson Act will remain unfulfilled, at least for us. One distant-water fleet, they realized, is the same as another, whether foreign or domestic.

It was against this backdrop that Peter Schmidt, George Fulton, and a few other visionaries at Marco came up with the *Storm Petrel* to fill the bill as a modern trawler built to deliver on shore. She was tanked and refrigerated in a whole new way so that the catch could be sorted into eight refrigerated seawater tanks through an ingenious system of bins. They put an articulated stern ramp on her—Fulton's patented design—and made her gantries and net reels easily removable so that she could pot-fish for crab or pack salmon to pay the bills while the shore-based industry evolved.

The *Storm Petrel* packs about 240 tons in her eight tanks—that's a half-million pounds—and routinely hauls back bags of 45 to 70 tons. She's outfitted with trawls and 5.5-meter alloy Super-Vee doors from Gary Loverich at Nor'Eastern Trawls. She also carries an extra set of doors, Super-Vee combos, that aren't as heavy as the 5.5-meter set. The smaller pair provides for better spread in shallower water but will not fish as deep. The winches are of a new, high-pressure design to test auto control and warp tension managed by a computer, a one-of-a-kind pair built by Marco.

"We never had any trouble with the winches until a year ago, and since then it's been one thing after another," Lloyd tells me. "We're going into the yard for a new engine in May, and we'll rebuild them and reposition them on the mid-deck." Marco did a similar refit of the *Sea Wolf* two years ago. "The idea is to go from being a good boat to being a hot boat," Lloyd says.

The *Storm Petrel* came out of Marco powered by the Cat 399T, an engine that was the equivalent of the square sail to the Vikings. Everybody seemed to have one, and they worked just fine; but now, with bigger nets and doors that characterize fast-paced pelagic (or midwater) trawling, everybody wants and needs more power. Because the complicated plumbing for the *Storm Petrel's* tanked refrigeration system packs the midship space, the yard crew will have to remove hull plates forward to get the old engine out and a new Cat 3516 in.

The *Storm Petrel* made her first few trips out of Kodiak in 1981 (I was aboard on one of them), delivering to the state-subsidized plant at Gibson Cove, formerly owned by the then recently defunct New England Fish Company. That experiment dragged on for a year, and though the Johannsons solved a few problems with the equipment and methods, the operation never became profitable without the subsidy. Out of necessity, the *Storm Petrel* jumped on the joint-venture bandwagon in the winter, packed salmon in the summer, and stayed in business.

In 1986, Pan Alaska sold its share of the boat to the Johannsons, who would manage and run her, with Peter Schmidt staying in the partnership as an owner. And so the *Storm Petrel* became a Norwegian family boat.

The Johannsons are best known for the *Oceanic*, and they also have another Marco, the *Commodore*. The latter came out of the yard in 1986 as a pure joint-venture trawler with no hold space at all, operating, as do most joint-venture boats, by transferring their catch to the foreign-processing ship directly from the water in whole cod ends. They also fished the *Storm Petrel* in joint ventures until they got their market with Alyeska.

Fixing a Winch

As Lloyd Johannson twists the filler cap off the winch housing, he is sprayed from head to toe by a sheet of pressurized hydraulic fluid. Clearly, a hose or valve has let go inside. In a reverse bucket brigade, the crew painstakingly empties about sixty gallons of fluid from the winch and then sets to work finding the break in the line. The problem turns out to be a cracked hose coupling. The repair goes slowly because the men are frustrated by the cramped confines of the winch housing and the lack of the right-size connector nipple. We jog into a building sea for four hours before the job is done, and by then the *Morning Star* has loaded up and gone to the plant. This puts the *Sea Wolf* ahead of the *Storm Petrel* in the rotation, and it means an extra day at sea for me and the crew.

Finally, we are back on the fish as the afternoon light begins to cast long shadows on the deck. The crew sets out the big super-mesh rope trawl and retires to the galley for their first food since the winch let go. Inside, dry and warm, the five hands settle again into the work-rest-work routine of the trawlerman. The pollock have scattered, and the fishing has slowed down from the dip-and-go tows of the heart of their spawning season, so the men know they'll have a reasonable break before hauling back. And because the busted winch has thrown the *Storm Petrel* out of the delivery rotation, Lloyd knows he has to pace himself so as not to arrive at the dock when the plant crew is busy with one of the other boats.

"I guess that's the end of the ten-minute tows," says deckhand Odd Olsen. "If you want to show trawling," he tells me, "take a picture of us in our bunks."

"This place is starting to look like a bus stop," says another hand, Bobby Johnson. At the galley table, the crew is reading magazines and picking through the bacon left over from breakfast. A James Bond movie with the sound turned way down is playing on the TV/VCR built into the bulkhead, but talk is more interesting to everyone still wired from the winch job. The walls over the horseshoe settee are still decorated with a set of plates made by George Fulton's wife, Muriel, that I remember from my first trip aboard here in 1981 during the Kodiak experiment. Each plate shows a different species of sea creature, beautifully drawn by Muriel and baked into the plate. The Johannsons have added a familiar plaque from the *Oceanic*: "Dear God, be good to me, the sea is so wide and my boat is so small."

The Crew

Aboard the *Storm Petrel* are Lloyd, Odd, Egil Mikkelson, and relief skipper Uthelius Storoy, all kin to the Johannsons. The crew on this trip also includes engineer Tom Sandel and deckhand Bobby Johnson, both locals from Dutch Harbor.

Born in New Bedford, Lloyd, twenty-eight, is one generation removed from Norway. "I've been coming up here [to the Bering Sea] since I was ten, but really fishing since 1979. I spent four years on deck crabbing and four years on deck trawling." The 1988 season is Lloyd's first as a skipper, and, like many other fishermen these days, he is building sea time to upgrade his license to higher tonnage. He flew up from Seattle with Odd a week before this trip, after a month-and-a-half break. "At first, nobody wanted to do this," Lloyd says of shore-delivery trawling. "But it's a fishery you can live with." Now the *Storm Petrel* has a multiyear contract with Alyeska.

Odd Olsen, who is in his late thirties, started fishing out of Atlantic City, New Jersey, then moved to Cape May, and finally, ten years ago, came west to the Pacific. Back east, he did six years on the Victor. Both he and the other "family" hands on the *Storm Petrel* seem to take pride in having been on the boat for a long time, a characteristic common to shoreside boats as compared with the grab-and-go you frequently find on the really high-bucks joint-venture boats and crabbers.

Like Odd, Egil started fishing on the East Coast, out of New Bedford. He came to the Pacific thirty-five years ago to tend salmon traps as a watchman, and he has gillnetted on Bristol Bay. Uthelius is aboard for a warm-up before taking over the *Commodore* in relief. He fished for thirty years out of New Bedford, twelve of them on the ninety-nine-foot *Valkyrie*. "What we call good bottom back there we don't even fish out here. It's too rocky," he says of the difference between the Atlantic and Pacific grounds. "There's that and the amount of fish—lots more out here. I've taken more beatings on the Atlantic, though; it's a tough ocean. Here, you're usually within a few hours of some harbor. On

Georges Bank, you're 200 miles out, so you can't do anything but sit there and take it."

The Legacy of Harold Fairhair

Lloyd's father, John, and the family crew come from the island of Karmoy, a place described in guidebooks as a "flat, barren island" off the southwest coast, which, during the time of the Norsemen, was the home of Harold Fairhair, one of the great Viking kings. Harold established a stronghold kingdom on Karmoy and the surrounding mainland fjords, and he forced many lesser chiefs to leave the country. He had nine sons who reached manhood, and his eldest and successor, Eric Bloodaxe, had eight sons. It's no wonder they wanted more land. Some of Harold's sons settled the islands of the North Sea and the Atlantic, including the Orkneys, Shetlands, Faroes, Hebrides, and Iceland.

Now some 35,000 people live on Karmoy, which is about three miles long and a mile and a half wide. Its economy, based for centuries on fishing, farming, and the fruits of Viking exploration, now depends on North Sea oil and an aluminum smelter. "When I was a kid," a woman from Karmoy would later tell me, "we were used to fathers and brothers leaving for two or three years, and we'd never hear about them until they came back. Now you get on a jet and you're there in twelve hours. A lot of young guys went in the merchant marines and got somebody to sponsor them to the United States.

"Everybody from Karmoy is related, I guess. We all looked to America as a way to get away from hand-to-mouth. We stick together, and we aren't that open to other people. We're told to be tough and keep to ourselves."

Dutch Harbor Locals

Crewmen Tom Sandel and Bobby Johnson live in Dutch Harbor with their wives and children because they like it. "Everybody here is working hard, all the time, and there's always a sense of excitement," says Tom. "If you're oriented toward buying a house and settling down for a rest, though, Dutch is not the place for you." Tom and his wife, Martha, have a two-year-old son. "His first word was 'boat,'" Tom says. He and Martha figure to stay in Dutch for maybe a few more years.

Bobby, though, might never leave. He moved to the Aleutians five years ago, after three years in Kodiak. He's married to June, who cooks for the *Storm Petrel* crew on unloading days, and has two kids. Bobby tried trapping on nearby Umnak Island the winter before, and while he was there, a big earthquake hit. "It shook me out of bed in this little cabin I had. I grabbed my survival suit and headed for the door. I thought a terrible disaster had befallen the Chain, that this was the end of it all, and I had nobody to tell me different. My plane didn't show to pick me up two days later, and I was sure I was the last man on Earth," Bobby tells me.

"A lot of people choose to live in Dutch, and what they do is secondary to living here. We have red and silver salmon runs, one month of trapping, and two good months of hunting," Bobby says. "We're fortunate out here because we can go to work for a living like this anytime we want to. You can always work in Dutch.

"It's amazing," he says, "ending up here."

———

The Storm Petrel, Sea Wolf, *and* Morning Star *are still up in the Bering Sea, delivering pollock to shore plants. In the early 1990s, the fisheries council divided up the catch formally between the offshore and inshore fleets, entrenching forever what was once an optimistic dream for local fisheries. And Dutch Harbor is more of a permanent, thriving town than ever before in its history.*

The Resurrection of the *Rebecca B*

CODFISH LONGLINING ▪ GULF OF ALASKA, 1989

At the roller, the sodium lights have the same effect as a campfire: the glare is blinding out to about a hundred yards, where impenetrable blackness abruptly takes over. The contrast robs me of whatever vision I could ordinarily squeeze out of the night, so the sea lion cavorting right at the line of light and dark vanishes and reappears as if by magic. The massive animal, hoping for an easy meal, seems alert to the risk it takes by coming near a giant, flashing creature like the boat, so it takes advantage of the deception at the edge of the darkness.

Aboard the freezer longliner *Rebecca B* in February, the campfire illusion dissolves also because of the raunchy fishing smells embedded in the nylon of my deck suit and the gore around the roller. And on this remote bay that rips into the mountainous coast of Kodiak Island, I can look down past the rollerman and see several fathoms into the Gulf of

Alaska. There, shimmering, a parade of fish spiral up from the depths in alternating flashes of ghostly white and brown, turning at the ends of the gangions attached at intervals to the ground line.

On the hooks coming over the roller are Pacific cod (which are gaffed because they are the money fish), pollock, an occasional conger eel, the squirming purple and yellow mush of starfish, small flounders so similar in size that they seem to have been pressed out by a cookie cutter, and, once in a while, a halibut. When a halibut comes up, skipper and rollerman Michael Fitzgerald stops the hauler and releases the big flatfish, which usually makes a muscular lunge down and away from the light, unharmed.

Landing a halibut in February would be a grossly illegal act, almost a political gesture, and if a fisherman is caught with one aboard, he is fined and suffers righteous indignation from other fishermen and fishery managers. The Americans are taking over the fishing grounds off Alaska, and they're bringing with them rules for fishing that struggle to equitably protect fish from fishermen, and fishermen from each other, while delivering good seafood at a fair price. It's a tall order.

Longliners, trawlers, and crabbers are pitted in classic, primal competition for a finite number of animals, and since the Magnuson Act began the banishment of foreign fleets from U.S. grounds, it's Americans against Americans. Many generations of longliners from the northern islands of the Japanese archipelago made this trip into the eastern and central Gulf of Alaska, though, dominating the grounds until the 200-mile zones became international law. The Japanese were among the first to begin the retreat, and the last to be finally gone. The already up-and-running American longline ice-boat fleet, composed of boats up to seventy feet long, didn't face the enormous development costs that faced the American factory trawling fleet, which took five more years to displace their foreign counterparts. By the early 1980s, American black cod longliners from Seattle, Sitka, Petersburg, and Kodiak were already claiming the eastern Gulf for that species, chasing out the Japanese.

Pacific cod, a different species altogether than black cod, kept the bigger Japanese freezer longliner fleet in business in U.S. waters until 1988. Now, even they are gone, replaced by a similar number of American freezer longliners like the *Rebecca B*. Each of these high-endurance, efficient boats ranges in size from 100 to 160 feet, and all are simple statements of catching and processing efficiency. They can produce high-quality, hook-and-line-caught fish in enough volume to justify long trips and a higher initial investment than smaller longliners that ice their fish and make shorter trips. Automated longline systems that can bait, set, and retrieve up to 20,000 hooks per twenty-four-hour day further increase the efficiency of the freezer longliners.

Pacific cod is critical to the success of any freezer longliner because black cod and halibut—the other longline species of choice—are hammered by such large fleets that the seasons are only days, sometimes hours, long. Though some fishermen change hooks and gear to get in on those limited fisheries, a year-round operation simply demands success with Pacific cod, a.k.a. P-cod, gray cod, true cod, or just plain codfish.

Fishing Smart

The working noise aboard the *Rebecca B* rescues me from the far less immediate concerns of international fishing politics. Against the background of mainstream rock-and-roll blaring from the shelter deck speakers, I hear the hydraulic farting of the hauler and the clicking of hooks into the racks of the Mustad Autoline system, which is a slave driver to the crew of five. As the ground line comes aboard, a device called a crucifier rips the hook from the fish's mouth, the fish drops into a bin, and the line, with hooks and gangions still attached, continues through the main hauler. It then moves down the deck for a three-foot run through a heavy pipe channel and rises to the combination hauler, which untwists most of the gangions with an ingenious water jet that one crewman calls the most amazing part of the system.

Then the humans are pulled into the machinery, so to speak. Resting against scarred wooden slats that are braces more than seats, three of the crew make sure that each run of line between gangions is hung cleanly on the rack, that each hook is still a viable catching device, and that the hooks are sharp, properly stowed, and free-running in the racks. For Pacific cod, they use very light, J-shaped hooks that bend under the strain of a heavier species like halibut, which they don't want to catch anyway; for black cod, they go with the Easy-baiter, a hook shaped midway between the J and the circle hooks; for halibut, they use the circle hook.

At several points in the hauling and racking of the line, a mistake can foul the entire set. Though the tedium is numbing, some corner of the mind must always remain alive and alert through the hours and hours of hauling, many of which are at night. Through it all, the crew carries on the kind of banter familiar to most men and some women from participation in team athletics such as football, in which the common pain and suffering create a bond. The players—like this crew—develop not just an idiom, but an entire language, and for hours sustain a cartoon of conversation rather than conversation itself. Their banter is full of playful but occasionally pointed insults, and it is absolutely necessary to survival on the processing deck of a distant-water longliner.

I hear the screech of the heading saw behind the roller, a distinctly final sound, made as one of the crew performs the mortal cut on each codfish. The saw's sound is *hmmmmmm-zing-hmmmm* as the blade first hits soft flesh, then the bone of the spine, then flesh again. The onboard processing cycle begins there, at the saw, and ends in forty-pound bags in the freezer holds in the belly of the boat, producing a fair income if the crew is successful.

To this point, in the history of this particular crew and this particular boat, success has been evasive for a variety of both wild and predictable reasons. Tonight, success and failure seem to have become a matter of just how firm the thawing squid must be to work properly in the automatic baiter. No bait, no fish—it's that simple. But the hope tonight is for more than just a lot of cod. If hooks without fish come up with bait still on them, even that's very good, because it means a high percentage of the squid made it to the bottom, where the fish are. Every set in the two days since leaving Kodiak has seen improvement in the percentage, and the sets of this afternoon were made with excellent cod sign on the fish finder.

The problem with squid—a change from the easier-to-bait but less-effective herring—has been getting a high enough percentage through the chopping and baiting end of the system. The idea is to hit about 95 percent and run 15,000 to 20,000 hooks in every twenty-four-hour day to produce 10,000 pounds of finished, bled, frozen Pacific cod. No one aboard doubts that this will come to pass, but irony crackles through the boat because the sophistication of the automation so obviously depends on the very hit-or-miss determination about the firmness of the bait. Everybody, though, knows it is only a matter of time before they figure out the squid.

Rebecca B and the Family

The *Rebecca B* is owned by Ron Hegge, a lifelong fisherman in his middle forties, soft-spoken but clearly enthusiastic about what he does for a living. He enjoys the puzzles of fishing and he has come aboard for this trip in February to fine-tune the boat and crew to catch Pacific cod, which is the mainstay of his year-round operation. His is a family company, based in Sitka, with his wife, Kathy, managing the accounting, expediting, and everything else ashore, and his son, Matt, running another one of his three boats and building equity in the company.

The crewmen of the *Rebecca B* have been together for about a year, fishing black cod and halibut, and they show the promise of a fine, young major-league infield that hasn't quite mastered the subtle rhythms of the around-the-horn double play. Their job isn't easy, not only learning to use the autoline system, which has been aboard for less than a year, but also getting in synch with the processing and freezing routine. Hegge purposely stayed with the more familiar long-line tub gear in 1988 because he didn't want his crew to be burdened with much more than the unfamiliar terrain of a new boat.

Everything about Hegge and his approach to fishing is upbeat and clever, and he reveals little of the strain of a man who has increased his financial and operational exposure by about 500 percent in one year. One of his favorite sayings—I first heard it when he was talking about coiling line—is "You have to be smarter than what you're working with."

Hegge migrated to Sitka in 1983 from Newport, Oregon, where he started fishing as a teenage sportsman and turned pro in a dory. He has gillnetted, trolled, and crabbed, and he came to Alaska for the most obvious of reasons: because that is where the fishing is still good. Almost immediately upon his arrival, he went into longlining, and his success at it brought him up through a succession of boats to the point that he now owns four—a fleet. And his fleet has one hell of a history, too.

Hegge and his son had a very productive longliner, the fifty-seven-foot *Michelle Ann*, with which they caught the crest of the black cod and halibut waves. Matt, in his early twenties, already had a decade of fishing experience and was a fully qualified skipper, and the family was ready for a second boat. So, in the fall of 1987, Ron went boat shopping. He has in-laws in Florida (one of them is aboard the *Rebecca B* now), and he was poking around yards and harbors down there looking for a bargain when he got word that the Finance Authority of Maine (FAME) was about to auction off three longliners at a bank in Rockland, Maine.

The *Rebecca B* and her sisters, the *Jessica B* and the *Cecily B*, were the first of the Woodin and Marean–designed steel seventy-six-footers launched in 1985 by the renowned Goudy and Stevens shipyard. The boats were conceived by and built for a man named Snelling Brainard, a Boston financier who brought, for a brief time, the marketing strategies of real estate development to the North Atlantic fleet, though he discovered that longliners are nothing like shopping malls.

With the kind of fanfare usually reserved for shopping mall openings, Brainard and his assorted interlocking corporations, doing business as Seabank Industries, announced a new age for the Atlantic fisheries. Using equity raised from a substantial cadre of investors, Brainard planned to populate several New England ports with fleets of automated longliners. These boats would work the historic but now-less-than-booming grounds more efficiently than the region's customary trawlers, which were barely able to pay their costs. He would do it, he said, because the higher-quality, longline-caught fish would bring bigger profits, because the seafood industry generally was in a steep upswing, and because he would build great fishing boats.

Like many fishing lures, Brainard's plans worked better on buyers and investors than on fish. He also attracted public financing in the form of loan guarantees from FAME, but that move switched the lights of accountability on bright. Brainard, though, apparently didn't understand the operations end of fishing as well as he did the front-end public relations and fund raising. Part of the problem, of course, was the fact that the fishing grounds off New England had been hammered by fleets and coastal populations for 200 years, and the fish were disappearing. In short, Seabank came apart like a dynamited hulk a year after the first hooks hit the water in 1985, went bankrupt, and so the boats were on the block.

"The auction was really something," Hegge tells me aboard the *Rebecca B.* It was held in the basement conference room of the Key Bank in Rockland, with about sixty people packed in for the two hours it took to dismantle Brainard's fleet. Only six people were actually bidding. "The *Rebecca B* was up to $340,000," Hegge says, obviously enjoying the memory of the moment's excitement. "I talked to my son, Matt, who's my partner, and said, 'I think the next $1,000 will do it,' and he said, 'Go ahead.' Walking up there with the check was really something." The roomful of people, he told me, broke into applause.

"Once we got into this one and found out how good and functional she is, we decided to go for the other two that had been sold to other people at the auction," Hegge explains. "I got together with Harold Thompson of Sitka Sound Seafoods on the *Jessica B* and the *Cecily B*. We paid the same price for the Jessica, but by the time we got to the Cecily, more buyers were interested, so she was a little more."

The *Rebecca B* was on the Pacific grounds in the summer of 1988; the *Jessica B* in December 1988; and the *Cecily B* in March 1989. (The *Cecily B* had become the *Melissa Beth* under her second owner, a Montauk, New York, longliner, but Hegge changed her name back to the original.) Under Hegge's hand, it became apparent that the boats were not the reason Snelling Brainard went broke. They are fine examples of a breed of fishing machine that evolved out of proven European designs adapted by solid American marine architects and builders. With plenty of attention to accommodating the automated longline system, crew comfort, and fish handling, these house-aft boats seem perfectly suited to the fishing chores at hand while effortlessly tending to the mariner's prime concerns of sea-keeping and safety.

For propulsion and auxiliary power, they are fitted with MAN diesels set in a forward engine room vented through distinctive foredeck stacks. The accommodations and working spaces are on three levels: the wheelhouse; a fully sheltered deck for setting, hauling, and processing; and crew quarters for eight farthest below. A skipper's stateroom is located off the wheelhouse, to the stern. The crew's quarters, placed low in the hull and far from the engines, make for an easy, quiet ride while recharging the vital human batteries. Built as pure longliners, the boats are compact and maneuverable, desirable qualities for staying lined up with the gear, with a setting port in the stern and a hauling port on the starboard side of the shelter deck. The boats have articulated rudders that answer the helm with a snap of the bow. The *Rebecca B*, I know, has a long, easy roll, dampened by stabilization tanks, and, though small for the worst weather the Gulf of Alaska routinely delivers, she'll be working near enough to shore to hide out during the most dangerous storms.

Freezing at Sea

Under the Seabank flag, the three sisters were ice boats, but the first thing Hegge did was add freezers. In the remote latitudes of the Gulf of Alaska, iced deliveries could not serve the high-quality Japanese market Hegge secured for Pacific and black cod. (Hegge does ice halibut because the seasons are only days long.) The boats remain identical, even with Hegge's modifications. At dockside in Seattle, crews installed deck cranes; ground tackle, including operable anchors and winches; and, among the finer details, trash compactors. The compactors came as a special deal at cost from a program in Oregon to encourage fishermen to reduce marine debris.

Each boat now has a quick-freezer on the shelter deck, just aft of the roller and heading saw. It can handle 10,000 pounds of finished product per day. The fish are frozen in pans according to size and grade, and then transferred to specially made and marked paper/ polyethylene bags, each holding about forty pounds. Hegge also added low-volume blast freezers to refrigerate the holds. The timing of the freezing process is critical; a whole day or trip can be lost if the fish are held too long before freezing or are frozen too slowly. The flesh of Pacific cod, particularly, is sensitive to timing during freezing; it crystallizes into worthless mush unless handled perfectly.

The standards for fish are set by the market, and Hegge's Japanese buyer sent a technician aboard for twenty days of trials and training when the first boat reached the Gulf. Pacific cod can be held no longer than six hours before freezing, a critical variable when timing the setting and hauling of the gear. The cod must be brought to 32°F as quickly as possible, and from there to 23°F in no more than two hours. The hold must be kept at −15°F. Twin generators power the freezer compressors to reduce the chance that a load could be lost to a thaw through a main engine breakdown.

Hegge is no stranger to the considerations of quality aboard a fishing boat. Soon after moving to Sitka, he became the director of

Alaska's Longline Fishermen's Association, a member of the Advisory Board of the North Pacific Fishery Management Council, and a member of the board of the Alaska Seafood Marketing Institute. The institute, particularly, was pushing quality and riding the rolling seafood marketing wave. "One of the things I like most about Alaska," Hegge says of his activities ashore, "is that it just sits there with open arms for anybody who is willing to get involved."

Aboard a freezer longliner, every member of the crew is constantly aware of the condition of the freezer. Those on watch keep time, check refrigerant levels and conditions, and monitor the temperature faithfully. The fish in the freezer are money in the bank, money that can turn into a worthless, foul-smelling pile of garbage if you don't pay attention to it.

The Fishermen

The crew aboard the *Rebecca B* are young, all under thirty. Michael Fitzgerald, the skipper, started fishing with his father on a troller off the Washington coast. He worked his way onto a tender and then took up longlining as if he were born to it. He is as familiar with the Gulf of Alaska as he is with Ballard, the section of Seattle known for Norwegians and fishermen, where one of his running buddies was Matt Hegge, Ron's son and the skipper of the *Jessica B*. Now they are competitors and teammates in that peculiarly American athletic sense. As we haul gear in Sitkalidak Bay, Matt is at the Alaskafresh Seafoods dock in Kodiak unloading 90,000 pounds—a full hold—into freezer vans bound for market. Michael is spending hours at the setting port and bait locker, trying to figure out his bait.

The rest of the *Rebecca B* crew (they are a man short this trip) are Rick Abbott, a skier from Crystal Mountain, Washington, whose specialty is setting his own hair on fire with a Bic lighter; Mark Bellon, from Missoula, Montana, who is the Nintendo king on the boat; Bob Edwards, like Hegge, from Newport, Oregon, a quiet man with

an easiness about him during the long, long hours of hauling and set-
ting; and Tim Sanger, Hegge's brother-in-law from Sarasota, Florida.
Sanger left the familiarity of a warehouse job to sign aboard for the
Alaskan grounds when Hegge was bringing his boats through the
Panama Canal.

This crew is making its second Pacific cod trip. Their first, which
began in late January, was marred by a learning curve steep enough
to cause nosebleeds. Everything about the Mustad Autoline system
was new to them, even the descriptive language: you talk about
"racks of gear," which hold 1,500 hooks, for instance, instead of
the traditional "skates of gear," which refers to lengths of ground
line. The ill-fated Seabank crews had taken the Mustad systems off
at the end because they couldn't keep up with the number of hooks
and couldn't hold experienced men who could operate them as the
ventures crumbled. Who wants to work on a boat headed for the
auction block?

The automated systems, though, are critical for Pacific cod. "I
talked to most of the crews and a couple of the skippers in Maine,"
Hegge says. "A lot of them have called to ask for jobs. They all liked
the boats and systems, but they told me they couldn't get enough volume to make any money under Brainard's business plan." Seabank had
projected 230 fishing days per year at 10,000 pounds of finished product per day, for a gross of a million dollars per boat per year. Hegge,
however, plans for 200 fishing days at the same 10,000 pounds per day
of Pacific cod, with additional income—but no more days—coming
from halibut and black cod.

Hegge's crews share out under set percentages and pay only for
their food. The price of Pacific cod in the form Hegge is delivering
ranges from $.60 a pound to $1 a pound; so shares for a full load of,
say, 90,000 pounds off a twelve-day trip will be worth the trouble of
learning the man-killing business of setting and hauling 15,000 to
20,000 hooks in twenty-four hours.

Bad Luck

The *Rebecca B's* first trip began with very few days of fishing due to the hideous weather this winter. Then, just as the crew members were beginning to get the hang of the system, they were touched by the fisherman's greatest tragedy. They'd been hanging on the hook in a remote bay out on the Alaska Peninsula, waiting out the weather in mid-February, when Fitzgerald decided to run in to Sand Point and wait it out there instead. Abeam of Devil's Bay, to the southwest of Chignik, somebody noticed a rescue-orange heap on the beach. It took form, in the binoculars, as a body in a survival suit.

Fitzgerald called the Coast Guard and drew as near as he dared to the rocky shore. He couldn't determine whether the body in the suit was dead or alive, so he made the only decision he could under the circumstances: somebody from his crew would fight the sea to shore. If the body were dead, the crew of the *Rebecca B* would bring it to Sand Point; if alive, they would perform a miracle rescue. So in his survival suit, Rick Abbott swam to shore with a line. There, he found a dead body lashed to a log and in pretty bad shape. Abbott decided that he wanted another line, that he did not want to return to the boat towing the body in his hands. He passed that message to the *Rebecca B*, and Tim Sanger swam another line to the beach.

Shaken, the men returned to their boat and confronted the reality of the badly decomposed body in the survival suit. The man apparently had been a member of the crew of the crabber *Vestfjord*, or so it said in a word on his suit: *VESTFJORD*. During a vicious assault of wind and cold that fishermen on the Gulf were calling the worst in memory, the *Vestfjord* had gone down a few weeks earlier under a deadly load of ice. She got off a Mayday, but no EPIRB signal was ever heard. The search for survivors went on for days; the Coast Guard and other boats came up only with some debris confirming that the *Vestfjord*, owned and crewed by men known to everybody in the Seattle fleet, had indeed been lost.

And now this. Doug Harding, the man on the beach in the survival suit, was thirty-five years old when he died. (I learned that later from the state troopers.) The crew of the *Rebecca B* found him in his final rest 170 miles from the search area.

"We were all pretty freaked out," Tim Sanger tells me. "He had obviously been alive in the water long enough to tie himself to a log. We got him aboard; I think a couple of us said prayers for him. It was a bad time."

The demoralizing effect of finding the body of Doug Harding is not a topic of conversation among the crew of the *Rebecca B* while I am aboard, perhaps because fishermen cannot afford to dwell upon such eventualities. The first trip had ended badly, with no fish to speak of, and this is the second.

Murphy's Law

So now, on Sitkalidak Bay, Fitzgerald and his crew, with the owner aboard, have nearly come to terms with their Mustad system, with the temperamental baiter, and with the subtleties of thawing squid. In two days, they have put less than 5,000 pounds of cod in the hold, but they are on the fish and the baiter is working. The squid are staying on the hooks; they are learning how to handle it, and how soon to take it out of the bait freezer before a set—all those things about good fishing that seem simple but are really the result of painstaking trial and error, often at great expense. Unless something happens, in a couple of days the *Rebecca B* will have a partially full hold worth the run to Kodiak to unload.

Then something happens. Something else. On the gear, this night as the sea lion laughs at us from the edge of the light, the diaphragms on each end of the transmission's pneumatic shift actuator burst; the drive train can be engaged manually, but you can't work longline gear like that. Fitzgerald pulls the actuator, a foot-long cylinder, simple in concept but arcane in that absolutely nothing aboard the *Rebecca B* will do to patch the rubber diaphragms that hold the air controlling the shifter.

Working at a galley table in a tee-shirt that says "In Cod We Trust," Fitzgerald tries neoprene glue and rubber patches; somebody suggests condoms, which actually might have worked. The first patch lasts through hauling the final string of gear that's already in the water, but it is then obvious that we are going back to town. The time is after midnight, making it March 1 that morning, and Fitzgerald tells me he's glad that February is over because it's been the worst month of his life. He sets the wheelwatch schedule, turns the *Rebecca B* for Kodiak, and turns in, exhausted.

"Sometimes I hate it, but other times I love it," Tim Sanger tells me at dawn on the run home. He is on the wheel as we ease through calm seas at nine knots off a coast that inspires well-being just because you feel so lucky just to be seeing it. To the north, the snow-white peaks slip into the sea from crests that march like a saw blade across the unusually clear blue sky in the flat light of an early Arctic morning. In February, the sun glides in a low groove across the southern horizon, a mere rumor of heat and light.

"I was as green as they get when I got on this boat last year," Sanger says. "Now I know there isn't any other way to get the feeling I got when we caught 70,000 pounds of halibut in one twenty-four-hour opening. I looked down in the hold and saw all those fish and I realized that I caught every one of them. And then there's the paycheck. I guess fishing is kind of addictive."

After almost a week in Kodiak, pinned to the dock by weather so bad that it closed the airport and stalled the arrival of a new shift actuator, the *Rebecca B* sailed on her third trip. The crew delivered 90,000 pounds of Pacific cod in perfect condition a week later.

—⁓—

Ron Hegge became a longstanding member of the North Pacific Fishery Management Council, one of eleven people who vote on the rules for fishing off Alaska, and continues his work ashore on seafood quality. He lost one of his longliners in the Aleutians, though fortunately the crew

*survived. The Gulf of Alaska fleet of freezer longliners,
including Hegge's, had fully developed by the early 1990s
and leveled off at about thirty boats, each of which depends
for its existence on the still-healthy stocks of Pacific cod.*

Kelping for Crude

THE *EXXON VALDEZ* SPILL • PRINCE WILLIAM SOUND, 1989

In the years to come, Cordova seiner Tom Copeland will undoubtedly mention the weather when he tells the story about kelping for crude. He will talk about the sky, the mountains, and the calm, blue water. He will describe as glorious that morning in early spring when he, Kathy Halgren, and deckhand Mike Fugett set out to pump oil from Prince William Sound. Copeland will also tell you that ten days after the *Exxon Valdez* vomited 11 million gallons of Alaska crude on March 24, he just could not stand the fact that almost no oil had actually been picked up. And he will insist that you understand that the pain of this spill, the worst human-kindled ecological disaster in American history, will not be eased by money or the laying of blame.

The idea of simply running out to a boom set across the bay, pumping oil aboard his boat, hauling it to Valdez, and selling it back to Exxon came to Copeland for the most obvious of reasons: "Nobody was really considering cleaning it up; it's absurd to think you can pick up that much oil, and everybody knows that," he says. "But it's spring, and we're fishermen here. We operate on production; we don't do time cards and Exxon logbooks. We don't sign Exxon contracts that prohibit us from talking to the press like they wanted us to. We don't let them take our lives from us and tell us it's just money.

"I decided the only thing I could do was deliver 500 gallons of oil a day to Exxon in Valdez and tell the governor that I expected a bounty on it. We have the technology—just pumps and totes—and besides, it is wonderfully, spiritually healing just to scoop that shit off the water."

Outrage, Real Outrage

Tom Copeland has fished out of Cordova since the early 1960s, working the seasons from roe-on-kelp in May to the more evenly paced seine openings on pink salmon later in the summer. He has the *Janice N*, a nice forty-two-foot Little Hoquiam combo, and, until the spill, he was a board member of the Cordova District Fishermen's Union (CDFU). During the week after the Exxon disaster, the board voted to remove Copeland, who advocated not only immediate legal efforts to shut down the trans-Alaska pipeline, but also more aggressive gestures toward the oil industry, which had, apparently, taken his life from him. The CDFU board, it seems, could not accommodate his outrage.

Two public events precipitated Copeland's confrontation with the union's board. First, he stood up at a Cordova town meeting and asked U.S. Senator Ted Stevens two questions: "How much money did you receive in campaign contributions from the oil companies during your last campaign?" and "Do you intend to refuse such contributions in the future?" Stevens's angry response to Copeland was "First, none of your business, and second, no."

Then, after consulting with several attorneys, Copeland realized that the infringement on his life was severe enough to warrant his seeking injunctive relief from a court. His goal would be to shut down the pipeline until the owners were able to prove that it could be operated safely, and that included the tankers that haul the oil from the pipe head. Again he confronted a politician, this time Alaska Governor Steve Cowper, who agreed to listen to Copeland on a minutes-long walk to an airplane. Copeland told him, "Governor, either you can do it [shut down the pipeline] or I can do it. But it really is your job." As was reported widely at the time, Cowper considered such a shutdown, but he eventually refrained.

Copeland's position was vehemently disputed by Bob Blake, a fisherman and, for two decades, the major political leader of the CDFU and the other local fishermen's group, the Cordova Aquatic Marketing Association. "You affect everybody in Alaska if you shut down the tube," Blake told me at the airport. Arriving after ten days out of town, he explained, "I stayed around for a while, and I just couldn't take it anymore. The best thing fishermen can do is go to work, get involved, and keep the story in the media so the country sees how they're getting hurt."

After Blake talked to me, one of his friends told him about the fistfights in the union hall among fishermen who claimed Exxon had favored some over the others in the awarding of lucrative charters, which, for most, had replaced fishing for the foreseeable future. The rate was $1,000 to $4,000 or more per day per boat. Herring season had already been canceled, and some of the salmon runs were threatened; so the lure was obvious.

The union had, by then, successfully fought to have the gag clause removed from the cleanup contracts between the oil company and the fishermen. Gone, too, was a clause that would have used boat charter fees to offset future claims against Exxon. Blake's friend also told him about a union employee who quit that day because of threats from angry fishermen. "The place is coming apart at the seams," the man said of Cordova.

"I just decided to go kelping for crude," Tom Copeland told me the night before he sailed. "I've given up on the political process. I had to ask myself, 'If I'm out of the business of blaming people, what do I do?' And the answer is: 'All I want to do is pump oil off the water.'"

Kathy Halgren, Copeland's friend on this venture, is the skipper of her own gillnetter, the *Luna Sea*, and a veteran of fifteen seasons on Prince William Sound. "It just does my heart good to pump the oil," she says. "We should have every boat that can get to the slick doing just that, for themselves and to get at least some of the oil off the Sound."

Guarding the Hatcheries

Sadly, though, what people from Exxon, various governments, and contractors—including fishermen—have been doing since the 987-foot tanker hit Bligh Reef is purely defensive and profoundly disorganized. Bickering and distrust characterized everything in the early days of the so-called cleanup; armed guards manned the doors of government agencies and oil company offices in Valdez. The simplest logistical chores were nightmares of inefficiency and misplaced effort against a background hum of depression and suspicion. A steady stream of dead and dying animals deeply etched guilt and pain into long days of work. And as futility took over from whatever optimism fishermen and other volunteers had brought with them to the horrible scene, anger, greed, and the dark side of human nature took over.

"You've got people working at $16 and $17 an hour treating this like it's just another Alaska boom," one fisherman told me in Valdez. "It's hard to feel like you're doing anything, though, since the whole thing is just too big, too awful." Still, some oil was picked up incidentally while fishermen were tending the booms in defense of the big salmon hatchery at Port San Juan, and they won a token victory there.

At nine knots, it takes the F/V *New Era* about twelve hours to haul a load of absorbent boom from Cordova to the Armin F. Koernig salmon hatchery at Port San Juan. This facility, and its partners on Easter Island and at Cannery Creek, are owned by the nonprofit Prince William Sound Aquaculture Corporation (PWSAC, pronounced by locals as Pizzwack). This corporation was created by special legislation after local fishermen were going broke after years of failed runs in the 1970s. The corporation takes enough fish to pay expenses, but the rest of the salmon goes to the fleets. (The idea of stabilizing natural runs to promote economic stability, of course, is about as foolish as shipping oil around the world in ships. Populations of salmon are meant to rise and fall as their environment changes. The control of nature, we are learning, is folly, no matter its intent.)

Seeking stability and having been assured by the law that they would share in the bounty, the fishermen imposed levies on themselves to build and support the hatcheries. And, under the leadership of Armin Koernig, they built hatcheries that now produce at least half the annual pink and chum salmon runs on the Sound. In 1989, 46 million salmon were scheduled to return.

"We had nothing we could count on; we could go broke any year before the hatcheries, but the people here did it," says Gerry Thorne, skipper of the *New Era* and a man who has fished for fifty-one years on the Sound. "I started in 1938, when I was eight years old, in a skiff with one shackle of gear. My father fished in the sailboats on Bristol Bay, and he told me to stay here, on Prince William Sound. 'It's a death trap on Bristol Bay,' he said. 'Stay here.'" Gerry's sons now own their own boats; Gerry and his wife, Ina, are about to retire. On this sad day in April, Gerry and the *New Era* are under contract to haul fuel, supplies, and the diaper-white oil containment booms to the hatchery.

As we come abeam of Montague Point, our bow begins to break up the first oil sheen we've seen on the way from Cordova. The reddish-brown mass forms a teardrop shape, following our wake past the boat and then re-forming in giant patches behind us. "Here's what pisses me off," says Gerry, shoving three fingers in my face as we stand over the chart table looking at the area around Bligh Reef. "For three days it was right there by the tanker, and for three days they didn't do a damn thing."

He moves his hand west over the chart to Applegate Reef, in the path of the main body of oil. "There's where a prawn fishery used to be." The radio crackles, and we are listening to traffic from Port San Juan. "They're talking about air-dropping booms," Gerry says. "The oil must have broken through."

Exxon and other petro-business people refer to the oil as "product" on the radio and in press releases: "We estimate that approximately 250,000 barrels of product were spilled." Product on the water is referred to as "heavy," which means a mass several inches to a foot thick; "mousse," which is defined as a thick jelly of crude oil and water, often mixed with debris, kelp, dead birds, fish, and other animals, and the like; and "slick," which is the familiar shimmering light coat of oil on the surface.

"These people, these oil people, they lie for money and no other reason," Gerry says. "When I was a little boy, I wouldn't think of doing that. It makes a guy want to declare war on the U.S. government, too, for putting up with this for money. We ought to take the officials responsible and drag them naked through the oil, then put them up on the beach and let them try to get the stuff off. Don't kill them; make them think about it. And I want Hazelwood [the tanker's captain] out there drawing wages, cleaning up the beaches. Jail won't do anybody any good.

"It's pretty obvious that the oil company strategy on a spill like this is 'Out of sight, out of mind,'" Gerry says. "'Sink it' is all they've really thought of since they knew right away they wouldn't be able to handle it."

A volunteer cleaning oiled otters in Valdez had a different take on the tanker captain. "This thing is on every television in America, in the world, and people can clearly see what our hunger for oil really costs. This could wake us up, so I think of him as St. Hazelwood of the Reef, a martyr for the cause."

In the three days right after the spill, fishermen from Cordova and Valdez went to work as volunteers to protect the hatcheries. PWSAC had some money; it wasn't much, but at that point the money didn't really matter. Because they were intimately familiar with the currents and tides that would surely take the oil past the hatcheries on its way to the Pacific, the fishermen knew they had to act quickly.

A week after the spill, Exxon wrote PWSAC a check for $1 million and agreed to keep at least another million dollars in the PWSAC account to protect the hatcheries. The relationship between the oil company and the salmon producers is far from amicable, but the money allowed PWSAC to pay the enormous costs of finding, buying, and flying the protective booms to Cordova and Valdez. As the days wore on, the chartered fleet increased with boats like the *New Era* running supplies and towing containment booms to control the oil and keep it away from the precious salmon fry.

At Port San Juan, four booms were laid in stages across Sawmill Bay, home of the rearing pens for the juvenile salmon. This was the site not only of a big hatchery, but also of a major eddy in the outbound current that now included about 10 million gallons of stinking, poisonous crude oil. As of April 17, almost three weeks after the spill, the fry in the pens had suffered no visible damage, thanks to the round-the-clock campaign to fight back the oil. The fry are scheduled for release by May 15, and that timing is critical because the little fish have to find plenty of food for their initial growth surge before heading for the open ocean. To satisfy this need, they are instinctively compelled to look for plankton, which, generally, is most plentiful on the Sound in May. Nobody knows what the oil has done to the plankton.

What Have We Done?

One of the most difficult things for people to accept has been the crippling uncertainty about the effects of the oil on the food web. Quite simply, nobody knows what this much crude oil in this environment will do. "With something this big, of course, humans can't do much more than watch," says Robert C. Clark, Jr. He is a geochemist with the National Oceanic and Atmospheric Administration and serves as member of the state-federal team trying to get a grip on the long-term effects of the spill.

"Making a prediction of what's going to happen in Prince William Sound in two weeks or two months or two years is not something most scientists are comfortable with," Clark says. He has been working on the relationship between oil and the ocean environment for twenty years and did some of the Environmental Impact Statement work on the Alaska pipeline. In 1976, he published a paper that said in no uncertain terms that a spill like this one was going to occur.

I want to know about the specific effects on salmon, but he wants to talk about other things. We are on a crowded plane, and he talks over the buzz of the twin jets and nearby conversations, which all contain the words "oil spill." "I try to be somewhat realistic," he explains. "Accidents will happen, where humans are involved, and the record for moving oil out of here wasn't bad until now. The bigger questions come up, though," Clark says.

"Why, for instance, during the building of the pipeline, did the nation stay with a fossil fuel policy instead of pushing for alternate energy sources? Because of the powerful lobbying of the fossil fuel industries in the policy process. It's dollars today, even if they buy votes against fisheries. Landings worth $20 million don't stack up well against $20 billion in oil revenues. Somehow, it has been lost that fishing dollars can carry on into infinity if we treat the resource sustainably, while the oil bucks are a one-time deal. I don't know why this doesn't get through to people."

The thoughts Clark expresses seem to tire him, and he glances distractedly at the scientific paper on his lap. It concerns the ways in which pollutants genetically alter certain organisms, a discussion of the kinds of stress that can modify DNA. He has another paper, too, one on the legal requirements for documenting the water sampling he will do on the Sound. "The uncertainties are myriad," Clark says when the silence passes. "But after ten years of work on this, we've learned some things. We know a little bit about how the oil goes into the environment; we know more about how to handle dispersants; we know how some organisms metabolize oil—bottomfish can, shellfish can't; we've learned about sublethal effects. The food chain tends to be pretty robust, but specifics are uncertain.

"We're not sure what salmon will do when they encounter the oil. They sink when they die, so evaluating this will be difficult. Some fish may detect the oil and not avoid it; their senses may grow accustomed to it. We're just not sure. They're mobile, so maybe they can avoid it. In limited-scale tests, we found that the oil can affect their homing senses. Our major effort here will be to look at the food web, which can provide direct physical information about the fisheries. Physical mixing will determine how far into the water column the oil goes," continues Clark, "but the problem is going to be that with a spill of this size, you can get almost endless redistribution of the oil. Every tide will move a new oil spill off the beaches that have been oiled and into the water again."

An Uphill Struggle

By April 17, Exxon claimed to be picking up 2,300 barrels per day. The Alaska Department of Environmental Conservation and the Coast Guard said that maybe 1,000 to 1,800 barrels would be more like it. Teams sent to the beaches to perform the actual cleanup were pulled out after only one day's work at the hopeless task. Exxon said it had thirty-nine skimmers and 200,000 feet of boom deployed, with 450 people working full-time on the scene. More equipment and people were set to arrive, including as many federal troops as Exxon or the state of Alaska said they might want. But the truth was beginning to settle: people can't clean up the oil; only nature will do that, and it will take decades.

The unusually warm, dry weather and the Sound itself have already done far more to make the oil disappear than the people who spilled it after years of assurance that they wouldn't. The Alyeska Pipeline Service Company operates the pipeline under agreements with the oil corporations and their stockholders, who own the oil itself. When the pipeline was built, Alyeska officials said they could completely clean up a 100,000-barrel spill in less than forty-eight hours. After the *Exxon Valdez* spilled 250,000 barrels, photocopies of the failed Alyeska contingency plan for a spill were circulated among fishermen, who settled for black humor because there was no other.

Three weeks after the grounding on Bligh Reef, about 40 percent of the oil has sunk, evaporated, or been driven into the bays and onto the beaches of the Sound's western shores, where the coasts play a symphony with the mountains. The rest of the oil is on the move, a vile, gelatinous mass susceptible to currents and winds that, in their more benevolent roles, circulate nourishment in the Gulf of Alaska. If you throw a corked bottle into Prince William Sound, and it doesn't ground anywhere, odds are good that it will drift in a circle. It will pass within sight of Kodiak, Sitka, and Yakutat and move back to two large islands—Hinchenbrook and Montague—that guard the entrance to the Sound, and then return to Kodiak, and so on.

Immediate Pain

As of April 21, 1989, herring fishing had been closed in some of the districts around Kodiak Island, and the people there felt the chill not only of lost seasons but of lost faith. Draggers from Kodiak towed gear through the leading edge of the spill, hoping to break it up. The oil is turning the corner north, too, into Resurrection Bay and up into Cook Inlet. Most people preparing for the arrival of the crude express anger and frustration, a sense of just not knowing what to do.

Tom Copeland, Kathy Halgren, and Mike Fugett, though, knew what to do. They delivered a hundred 5.5-gallon kelp buckets of salvaged crude oil to Exxon in Valdez on April 11, receiving a bounty of twenty dollars a gallon. Exxon immediately began negotiating with

Copeland for a secured service contract, stipulating a daily fee plus a gallon rate, similar to a fisherman's marketing contract. I don't know whether Tom accepted the offer; phone lines to Cordova are jammed.

For a few weeks, Exxon's tanker, the angry fishermen
of Prince William Sound, and everyone's television sets
burned new grooves in our minds about what it really
costs each of us to drive to work every day. One
particular dawn as I stood in the wheelhouse of a boat
on the Sound, watching the sun rise over the grounded
tanker, a fisherman said something like this to me:
"I don't blame Joe Hazelwood or Exxon; I blame
everybody who is at the wheel of a car, commuting
this morning in L.A. or Chicago or wherever. Gas
doesn't cost a buck twenty a gallon; it costs this.
" For a while, things changed. But the new awareness lasted
barely a year. Exxon performed one of the
most revolting acts that followed the spill when it renamed
its tanker the Sea River Mediterranean
in 1990 and again sent her to sea.

Derby Days, Sleepless Nights

HALIBUT LONGLINING ▪ SOUTHEAST ALASKA, 1992

Abig fish wakes everybody up. It's three in the morning; the skipper at the roller hollers, "Gaff hook," to get some help with a halibut he can't handle by himself; and for a few minutes, the numbness goes out of the long night. Typically, the deckhands are lost in the bloody tedium of gilling and gutting in the too-white glare of halogen lights, wrestling the glistening fish against the roll of the boat in a sloppy chop. They respond instantly to the alert, though, stow their knives, grab their gaffs, and, with the scrambling grace of practiced motion, step cat-quick through the pile of fish to the rail.

Like the 5,000 other halibut crews at sea off Alaska at three in the morning in early June 1992, Dan Kowalski and Kurt Hoelting aboard the *Sue Ann* have been fishing without a break for fifteen hours. They are shivering in their own sweat under gore-splattered raingear, hungry to the point of nausea, and alternately giddy and silent with fatigue. This twenty-four-hour season—the Derby—is a grotesquerie of modern fisheries policy on which as much as half of their annual incomes depend, and so they endure. Some fishermen like the gamble, the quick money, the thick, primitive rhythms of this kind of competition; not many like the danger, the waste, or the dark hours of that long night.

Two days earlier, we had anchored at Read Island in Farragut Bay, on the eastern rim of Frederick Sound, to bait up, a grueling task like what I imagine repetitive prison work must be. Each of the thousands of hooks the crew will soon set on their longlines was sharpened, straightened, and baited with a piece of cut octopus or pink salmon. The crew, Dan and Kurt—a.k.a. Sven and Ole—are veterans, both in their forties. Dan has been a boat owner and skipper for fifteen years; Kurt a crewman for as long on many different boats in both the longline and salmon seine and gillnet fisheries. They gave each other the nicknames to allow their longstanding friendship to survive the onboard tensions and roles of skipper and deckhand.

This morning of the opening, I was the last to wake in the cramped fo'c'sle, reluctant to emerge from a waking dream in which we were in a sheltered cove, sharing it with enormous, ancient whales. They were the size of ships, and gnarly with barnacles, with very sentient eyes. I dove in the water and was snout to snout with the biggest one; then I got scared and dove under it, waking up as I drifted down under its enormous form, fracturing light into shafts and rings overhead. I felt no fear then, only a slight anxiety.

I woke fully and emerged into the wheelhouse to find Dan and Kurt donning raingear over clean sweatpants. Dan wore a hat; Kurt a hooded sweatshirt—standard fishermen's gear. On the cuffs of each of his orange rubber gloves, Kurt had written "RIO" with a black marker. I asked him why, and he told me he and Fritz Hull, a friend who was in Rio de Janeiro at the Earth Summit, had agreed that Kurt would send him thoughts of success and progress. The word "RIO" on his gloves would be a reminder as he worked here on Frederick Sound, cutting bait, rigging the skates of gear, fishing, and cleaning halibut during the mind-addling hours of the Derby. Dan dedicated his gloves, too, but to his two-year-old daughter, Julia.

High-Stakes Fishing

We cruised past Point Agassiz opposite Petersburg on the way out here, headed eventually for the grounds off Cape Fanshaw known as the "Ramp," a gradually shallowing slope ranging from 150 fathoms to 80 fathoms in line with the tidal flow that brings the fish "up the ramp." Dan calls the crowded scene at the Ramp the "Cape Fanshaw Fandango," after a nearby promontory.

As we head for the grounds, we do not really know what the millions of pounds of halibut will be worth to us or the rest of the fleet when we return to sell at the tenders and fish plants. The price rumors have thrown everyone into bad moods, though, with $.65 for smalls and $.90 for larges, respectively, less than half of last year's payday. A rush of Russian halibut imports, caught by wide-ranging American factory longliners, is to blame, according to the domestic packers, as well as the steady supply of Canadian halibut since the Canadians switched to year-round fishing with individual quotas. The Derby further hurts the quality of the fish because it arrives at the dock all at once and lowers the price, so the Americans in their own waters are at the bottom of the demand scale this year. The Derby is wide open, so just about anything that can float is pressed into service, and a lot of the greenhorns have no idea how to really care for halibut on the grounds. Cleaning and icing are critical, even in the short hours of the Derby.

But if your boat holds together, if you don't tangle hopelessly with the gear of another fisherman on crowded grounds, and if you find the fish, the payoff is thousands of dollars, cash, right now. If not, you can lose your boat because you can't make the payments, or maybe you struggle to make ends meet for a whole year, or make a bad decision under financial pressure. The Derby will physically wreck you for days after you return to port—small towns such as Petersburg, Kodiak, Sitka, and Dutch Harbor, where the tension and competitive angst lend a couple of weeks of range-war flavor to otherwise nice places to live. The Derby may, as happens more often than most fishing people like to admit, even kill you with an assist from a vagrant gale, an overloaded boat, or the grim consequences of a careless moment around the flying hooks, lines, and anchors that are the tools of your trade.

Once, in the pre-Derby days of the early 1970s, a halibut actually killed a fisherman one-on-one. Joe Cash, of Petersburg, disappeared at sea and was found later, lashed to the winch of his boat *Flicka*, awash on a beach, with a huge, gaffed halibut at his feet. In his battle to subdue the fish, Joe apparently fell, severed an artery, and bled to death with his halibut.

By 1992, the entire U.S. commercial fishery for Pacific halibut off Alaska had devolved to a pair of twenty-four-hour openings, one in June and one in September, during which enormous fleets on the Gulf of Alaska and Bering Sea landed about 65 million pounds of halibut. The policy that engenders the Derby blends wide-open access to the grounds with a fixed quota, inexorably shortening the seasons.

Most halibut landed by commercial boats are in the twenty-to-hundred-pound range, but often enough, a giant puts a whole crew to the test, appearing like the shadow of a barn door on the rising line. A longliner crew is a team, led by the skipper, with one to ten men and women working on deck, each with specific responsibilities. Great fish cleaners and fast baiters are treasures, and because the fishing is so physically demanding, youth and strength are hot commodities.

Landing a seven-foot halibut weighing, say, 300 pounds is anything but routine. The fishermen sink their T-handle, stainless-steel, hay-hook gaffs in the fish's head, with the skipper choreographing placement and everybody muttering and grunting things like "Nice, nice fish. Nice fish." A giant halibut is oddly docile alongside, even with two or three gaff hooks in its head, and the chore is really to lift the huge, muscular flatfish from the sea into the boat, a matter of sheer strength, and keep it calm once aboard. Among the odd truths about a halibut is that you can settle it down by rubbing its belly, the white side of the fish, right along its lateral line.

The fish will have sucked a hunk of bait into its cavernous mouth sometime during the hours since the two-and-a-half-mile-long groundline and its thousands of hooks settled with its anchors from the stern of the boat. If the fishermen prevail, the halibut will be worth its weight in dollars to them at this season's price. Later, the fish packer, broker, grocer, and restaurateur will make more money on its demise, and finally, somebody will enjoy a meal of its exquisite white flesh, which, most agree, doesn't really taste fishy. If the halibut gets away, well, so it goes.

All big halibut are females. A great she-beast like the one that delivered the crew's wake-up call metamorphosed from a drifting larva in the nourishing soup of the Gulf of Alaska about forty years ago, and would have kept growing until she died. Pacific halibut (*Hippoglossus stenolipis*, which means "horse tongue, narrow scale") are broadcast spawners, with each female squeezing hundreds of thousands of tiny eggs into the deep, open ocean, and each male contributing clouds of milt to the statistical breeding waltz. The fertilized eggs are near-microscopic specks and much more delicate than the eggs of most fish; the larvae are helpless prey. When a larva finally develops intestines, a mouth, and well-defined muscles that allow swimming, it assumes the familiar shape of the flatfish and its eyes migrate to the up-side, where they remain. A juvenile Pacific halibut, for its first year, inhabits the shallow water of the coastal zone, threatened by other sea creatures and the pollution incidental to dense human settlement at the water's edge. Its Atlantic cousin, *Hippoglossus hippoglossus*, is far less prolific these days due to centuries of fishing pressure and human incursion.

Bob Stickney, an aquaculturist at the University of Washington, has been working for two years on captive breeding of halibut, hoping to get a better grip on the nature of the fish and develop techniques to enhance the precious wild stocks. "I'm fascinated by them," Stickney says. "They start out among the most fragile eggs and larvae and develop into the toughest fish there is. We've never had a halibut spawn in captivity, but we have maintained postlarval fish. In a tank, they get docile and will eat out of your hand. I'm really attached to them. They'll come to the surface and look right at you."

The early settlers of the Northwest Coast, the seagoing bands of Haida, Tlingit, Tsimshian, and Makah, were fascinated by halibut, too, and bound practically and spiritually to the great fish. When the ocean calmed in the summer, they risked paddling offshore to catch them with stone-weighted lines of twisted sinew or fibrous bark and wood-and-bone hooks that bear a remarkable resemblance to the relatively new circle hooks used by contemporary fishermen. (The circle hook is twice as effective as the ordinary J-shaped hook because the force of the striking fish is leveraged to set the barb, as was the aboriginal hook.) The return of the halibut fishermen was cause for ceremonies, feasting, and myth making, and halibut appear often in carvings and tools as symbols of the superabundance of the era prior to dense human settlement.

Not surprisingly, the Pacific halibut almost went the way of the buffalo when American fishermen brought modern fishing methods, transportation out of the region, and European-style commerce at the end of the last century. Intensive fishing on the Atlantic had wiped out viable stocks of Atlantic halibut, an outcome cited often in support of the theory that humans will always abuse a resource held in common. As long as the locals of New England were the only customers for the halibut, the stocks supported the necessary fishing. Demand from markets in Europe and, via rail, other North American cities, however, induced fishermen and packers to overharvest, eventually reducing the catch rate to such a low point that there was no money in the fishery. For a while, fish peddlers sold bogus halibut, fillets of other flatfish that looked enough like the real thing to fool the uninitiated.

But the demand for halibut continued, so it was inevitable that word of virgin grounds off Washington, British Columbia, and Alaska trickled back to the New England fleets. The crewmen of the seventy-nine-foot sailing schooner *Oscar and Hattie* were the first to risk the 15,000-mile voyage around Cape Horn, and the gamble paid off. In the fall of 1888, they shipped 50,000 pounds of fresh, iced halibut back east by rail from Tacoma, Washington, a bonanza that triggered a boom.

Big company steamships that carried fleets of sail- and oar-powered fishing dories soon took over from the adventurers; landings of more than 300,000 pounds per ship became common; and over the next four decades the fish steadily disappeared. According to current proponents of the theory of the "tragedy of the commons," the mobility of the fishing fleet, coupled with open access to an unlimited resource, created an expanded common pool of the fish required by a certain market niche.

The exploitation of common property resources to the point of destruction can be ended by applying one of three principles of social engineering. One is to ensure that the resources remain true commons of reasonable size, managed by local people for their own use, a possibility that may no longer be practical with global markets. A second alternative is privatization, fencing grazing land, for instance, and granting ownership to individuals who then presumably will protect their property. This alternative effectively destroys the commons—not necessarily a desirable outcome, and one that is based on the pessimistic notion that humans always lay waste the Earth.

"The modern world does not quite realize what it has lost," writes Gary Snyder in his essay "The Place, the Region, and the Commons," an eloquent call for the recovery of the commons. "The commons is a level of organization of human society that includes the non-human. Understanding the commons and its role within the larger regional culture is one more step toward integrating ecology with economy. Bioregionalism is the way, on a large scale, to organize ourselves in the context of caring neighborhoods instead of detached, conflict-based economies."

The third alternative for ending abuse of commonly owned resources is administration by government authority, an undesirable outcome to many, particularly those who thrive on the frontier or the illusion of the frontier. In 1932, though, Pacific halibut were saved from decimation by the intervention of government authority in what has become an acclaimed stroke of resource management. The United States and Canada finally agreed to set quotas and enforce closures to end the uncontrolled harvest of halibut. The treaty created the International North Pacific Halibut Commission, which celebrated its sixtieth anniversary in 1992, with healthy halibut stocks in the waters of both countries.

"The U.S. and Canada reacted to the conservation threat fairly early in the game," says Steven Hoag, the commission's deputy director for the past twenty-five years. "Everybody knew the situation was critical in the thirties, and we had a close-knit, homogeneous fleet that got used to the idea of closures and conservation. Until the sixties, just about everybody in the fleets of both countries was of Norwegian descent, and it was kind of like a big family with a common problem."

The commission, with a staff of fisheries biologists, assesses the condition of the stocks and sets annual quotas to maintain sustainable yields. They enjoy the luxury of leaving to each country's managers the specific allocation decisions, out of which arise the most bitter conflicts in the fisheries. Nothing is tougher to say than "Fisherman A can catch ten fish; Fisherman B can only catch five," and therein lies the genesis of the Derby.

Until 1981, U.S. and Canadian fleets fished in each other's territorial waters, but the arrival of extended territorial jurisdictions and 200-mile exclusive economic zones ended that cooperative approach. At the time, the fleets were just about equal in size, with about 400 boats each and annual quotas that lasted most of a year. You fished when the weather was good and delivered every ten days or so to packing plants that were buying halibut anytime.

When the curtain fell on open waters for halibut, the Canadians retreated to their home waters off British Columbia with access to far fewer fish. The reaction of the Canadian government to home-waters fishing was to limit the number of licenses available to the fleet to the 430 that are now fishing. In 1990, the Canadians went a step further and created what they call the individual vessel quota (IVQ) system, awarding each vessel a specific percentage of the overall annual quota, based on past performance.

The United States, though, left the door wide open to new entrants into the halibut fleet, and by 1990, the owners of 7,000 boats ranging in size from outboard skiffs to 220-foot factory longliners held permits, about 5,000 of which are actively fished each year. So while the stocks of halibut are healthy, the fishery resembles a street fight instead of a respectful effort on the part of the community to gather food.

"In the early eighties, the longline fleet grew out of control for a couple of reasons," says Steven Hoag. "First, you have a lot of refugees from other fisheries that have been limited, like salmon in Alaska, coupled with an overall increase in population on the Pacific coast. And you can't discount the technical revolution that has made catching halibut a lot easier than it used to be in the early days when you had to serve a long apprenticeship just to know where the fish are and how to find them." Now anybody with typical wheelhouse electronics radar, depth sounder, plotter, tracker, and radios can navigate to the grounds and back and have a good shot at finding fish. Circle hooks just about doubled the fisherman's effectiveness, too, and recently developed snap-on gear doesn't require the skills needed to handle conventional gear with hooks permanently affixed to the groundline.

"It all adds up to a bad situation," says Hoag. "The halibut are in fine shape, but the commission and most fishermen now support some form of limiting access to the fleet. In Canada, though, they had a hard time coming up with a system acceptable to 400 fishermen. We're trying to come up with one acceptable to 7,000, plus thousands of men and women who work on crews but don't own boats."

When the clock struck noon on June 8, 1992, and the hooks began clanking out of the setting chutes on thousands of halibut boats, the possibility loomed that the United States might soon adopt a share quota system similar to Canada's. "I think those opposing a quota system are in the minority," said Hoag, echoing the observations of many in the fishing community. "It's a very vocal minority, though, and for some of them, open access is a bit of a religious thing, a 'keep government out of the Last Frontier' mentality."

The frontier mentality. Fisheries politics on the Pacific are particularly noxious because the men and women of the fleets and coastal towns are just a generation or less removed from superabundance, homesteading, and virtually ruleless resource extraction. Mixed feelings and bad blood divide entire towns, have ruined countless friendships, and provoked ugly confrontations on the grounds.

American consumers, who, after all, are the majority stakeholders in the halibut and all other common resources, generally welcome access limitation. During the Derbies, fish handling and processing isn't top quality simply because all the fish arrives at the same time. Year-round supplies of fresh halibut, black cod, and quota share species would be roundly hailed by middlemen and consumers, as year-round production of halibut from Canada is now.

A lot of people have likened limiting access to the fisheries to fencing the ranchlands of the West during the last century. Clem Tillion, a frontier character himself who homesteaded on Kachemak Bay and fished for a living, has been a highly visible political figure in the evolution of the fisheries. Ironically, he has led a decade-long campaign to impose a quota share system on the longline fisheries. "If we had kept the open range, it would have turned the grasslands into a desert. So, is it sad that we fenced it? Yes. Is it sad that we are fencing the ocean? Yes. Is it necessary? Yes. Is it the end of the Last Frontier? Yes. It is the very end, but the longer we wait, the more people are going to get hurt."

Tillion's grudging acceptance of the realities of a world in which a booming human population is competing for access to finite natural resources—particularly food—is typical in the fleets. "An IFQ [individual fisheries quota] system means I could own access to a certain amount of the halibut catch forever," says Petersburg skipper Dan Kowalski, who has been fishing for sixteen years. "That's cuckoo. But I'm for it because I started fishing halibut when you could work fishing into a reasonable life. With IFQs, I could fish fewer skates [strings of gear] for a longer time, maybe with my young son. In the Derby, that's not possible."

Kurt Hoelting, Kowalski's deckhand who has never owned a boat and never wants to, will not receive any free quota shares under the proposed plan, though he would be eligible to buy them. He nonetheless supports the new system. "This is a fishery out of balance. Our relationship with the fish is skewed to abuse, waste, and capital pragmatism, rather than respect and responsible harvest," Hoelting says. He is, by his own insistence, not "your average longliner."

"Most fishermen are tuned in to the bottom line, which is the health of the stocks," Hoelting says. "As long as a fishery is being managed, as this one is, for the health of the fish, I don't think much about anything except catching as big a chunk of the quota as I can. I'm sick of this way of fishing, though, where everything is on the line in one day."

Last year, during the September opening, another boat on which Hoelting works had to leave lots of gear on the bottom and run for cover when a gale blew into the eastern Gulf. "We went out two days later and shook 16,000 pounds of mostly dead halibut off our hooks and back into the sea. A whole fleet of boats in that area had to do the same thing. A few boats pressed on and hauled gear in the storm, but they were in serious, serious danger. The halibut that died for nothing on the gear we had to abandon would have been worth $3,000 to me alone," Hoelting says. "It was not fun, a big waste, and, all around, kind of a bummer."

Kodiak, one of Alaska's archetypal fishing towns, is a stronghold of opposition to any form of access limitation. They fought limiting entry to the salmon fisheries (which has proved to be a boon to both fishermen and the salmon) to the bitter end, and twenty years later some wounds haven't healed yet. Opponents say anything but wide-open access cuts off the opportunities for young fishermen, and restricts their ability to move between fisheries when some cycles are up and others down, but the most messianic among them say limiting access is just not the American way.

Many who oppose privatization with a quota share system object to the inevitable creation of an elite class of resource owners. Though current plans include shares that may be used only for fishing in waters near local communities, and some limits to how many shares a person can own, the consolidation of access rights is probably unavoidable.

"I switched my vote because I finally realized that less than 5 percent of the fishermen were going to end up with more than 50 percent of the total shares," says Larry Cotter, a former member of the federal council responsible for making the rules for halibut. "The guys with small shares are going to sell them, and they're out. I just have a hard time with this because once we do it, it's forever." The council is considering quota shares for another species, black cod, and is being carefully watched as a bellwether. So far, only one other federally regulated fleet, surf clammers off the Atlantic Coast, operates under a quota share system.

In midsummer 1992, the Secretary of Commerce, the Cabinet member responsible for federal fisheries, was reviewing the quota share system for halibut while lobbyists for both sides worked overtime on congressmen and bureaucrats. But even if the system clears the regulatory hurdles, there are sure to be further legal and administrative challenges. Meanwhile, for another year or two, the Derbies will continue.

"A fisherman's relationship with his boat, the bottom, the tides, and finding the fish is real good stuff," says Dan Kowalski. "I like the sea, the landscape, the fish, and getting paid for my work. But I don't like the Derby, crossing over other boats' gear, and the intense competition for space to set on the grounds. The pleasure goes out of it, and things seem out of balance.

"It's sad that society hasn't come up with a better plan for these fish and fishermen."

———〜〜———

Society did come up with a better plan, and the Derby of 1992 was the last of its kind. The following year, Dan Kowalski and other longliners who met certain historical requirements for landing halibut and black cod received shares of the annual quota in perpetuity. Kurt bought some shares, too, since crewmen qualify to own them, and he and Dan fish their shares together aboard the Sue Ann at a far safer, more leisurely pace. Dan was about to quit fishing to come ashore, but the share quota system has kept him, and his young son, who can now work with him, at sea.

Salmon in the Trees

LOGGING THE TONGASS ▪ SOUTHEAST ALASKA, 1999

"One of the great dreams of man must be to find someplace between civilization and nature where it is possible to live without regret."
—Barry Lopez

I'd better tell you right off that I have never seen spawning salmon actually *in* the spruces, hemlocks, alders, or any of the other trees in the rainforest that embraces the Alexander Archipelago. I *have* seen them in the creeks, of course, during the warm months when they arrive from the sea, vital and silver, only to turn into ragged monsters to surrender to their descendants. I take a one-two punch of mortality and renewal every time I stand on a muddy bank and watch those beautiful fish turn so poignantly into tatters right before my eyes, with their next generation tentatively on deposit in the streambed gravel. They disguise themselves and then disappear altogether, as though they are determined to blend with the moss, bark, silt, debris, and earth of the place.

It's hard to resist thinking of those fabulous, recently departed salmon as ornaments dangling from the branches of the trees, clattering around up there like wind chimes. Since we started to suspect that hacking down the rainforest would kill the salmon, it's important to know that trees need fish as much as fish need trees. And as it turns out, wishing that salmon really spawn in the trees of the miraculous bit of territory we call the Tongass isn't just a matter of having a hyperbolic imagination. At a potluck in Ketchikan a few years ago, a geologist showed up with hard evidence that salmon eventually do make their way into trunks, branches, leaves, and needles, especially the royal old-growths of the outer islands. The menu that evening was predictably delicious — baked halibut, hot dish, salad, and wine, the food of every winter anybody has ever spent in a Southeast Alaska town. The company was similarly comfortable, about a dozen of us who ate, then helped our hosts take some art off the walls for the slide show. Then, for an hour, we sipped decaf and wine while the geologist, an exuberant man named Jim Baichtel, told us about his enchantment with limestone karst of Prince of Wales Island.

His slides were portraits of lush trees and groves, clear-cut ridges, saddles and valleys, and people on claustrophobic expeditions into the labyrinth of caverns and tunnels that underlie the familiar surface terrain. In some of the pictures, spelunkers are hanging on ropes in deaddrop shafts more than 500 feet deep, grinning. In others, dusty cavers bathed in the glow of headlamps and strobes are wedging themselves through subterranean gaps barely as wide as their hips. They are equipped with special straps on their boots, Jim explained, to allow their comrades to extricate them when they get stuck. Over the rattling of the projector, he also told us stories about the geologic skeleton that shapes the archipelago and serves the trees and the salmon.

Imagine a braid of a half-dozen gigantic strands of ancient rock, winding along southwest to northeast line, like Rapunzel's hair wrapped together and laid against the continent. These six tendrils are the remnants of distinct terranes, pieces of drifting crust that docked against the old, old rock of the North American plate and fused together over the past couple of hundred million years. The rocks vary wildly in origin, age, and kind, but all of them seem to submit to two generalities: They were once buried deeply, then uplifted and exposed by glaciation and erosion; and their grain is consistently parallel to the long axis of the archipelago. A great fault, one of the most obvious and beautiful in the world, cleaves the entire assemblage in a fracture more than 300 miles long, now occupied by the waters of Chatham Strait and Lynn Canal.

To the east on the mainland lies what pioneer geologist John C. Reid called "a truly stupendous body of granite." We know it now as the Coast Range, the uncountable crags that pucker into the sky at the thoroughly unnatural border between Southeast Alaska and British Columbia. To the west, the island rocks are metamorphic and sedimentary melanges that include gneisses, schists, phylites, slates, limestones, and marbles. In most places, the limestone and marble are 10,000 feet thick, and the quarries at Tokeen and Marble Island have barely touched what is estimated to be 800 million tons of high-quality marble that would be the envy of any Renaissance sculptor. The four great columns in the facade of the State Capitol Building in Juneau are Tokeen marble, and from 1909 to 1932, more than a dozen quarries dispatched shipments of the rock around the world.

The point of Jim's entertaining explanation of the geology of the regions was to lay the groundwork for his argument against cutting the old-growth trees on the outer islands. If, he reasoned, the limestone karst could be as valued as the timber above it for recreation and research into the history of the place, there would be reason to stave off the logging juggernaut that threatened the trees. Under a set of Byzantine timber harvesting rules, the great trees of the world's last temperate rainforest were being cut and shipped to plants that turn them into chewing gum wrappers, beaverboard, and other pulp products. This so-called industry operates at a net loss to its owners, the citizens of the Tongass, the United States, and planet earth. It is subsidized by some of the foulest smelling legislative pork ever to come out of Congress accompanied by the bleat of "jobs vs. the environment" rhetoric. Some people rebelled, finally, like Jim Baichtel and others inside the United States Forest Service who are supposed to represent the best interests of the nation and the world. The men and women of the fishing fleets headed for the trenches, too, along with a lot of other people who grasped the complex dependencies of the Tongass. For a time, the chief strategy to counter the brute political muscle that kept the timber barons afloat was to demonstrate what was euphemistically called "multiple use."

The outer islands of the archipelago, Baichtel told us, very likely were among the first to emerge from the ice 10,000 or so years ago and some patches of terrain might even have remained ice-free throughout the cold times. They were refugia for animals including bears, deer, and salmon, and quite possibly humans who rode out some pretty rough times together or just moved through the remains of the island group on their way to better living to the south. Baichtel and others also figured that the relationship between karst, trees, salmon, and every other living thing is not well-enough understood to permit the removal of a single, terribly consequential element of this version of life's formula: the trees. The biggest, healthiest old-growth trees grow where they do because the porous limestone beneath a thin covering of soil and organic debris is nothing less than a massive storm drain. The karst filters the sweet, steady rain into caves, caverns, underground channels, and the sea.

The karst, the trees, the caves, the salmon, even the people, Baichtel said, are parts of an immensely interdependent, complex system about which we still know very little. The returning salmon definitely pack nitrogen and other essential ingredients of forest life in their bodies, and they surrender them year after year after year. The fish rot quickly, and find their way into the trees in the guts of bears, humans, birds, and other animals that leave their droppings in the forests. Eagles and osprey haul rotting salmon around like take-out waiters, depositing their remains in the uplands, where the porous understory and rock deliver the meal to root webs. I was reminded that night of a wry bit of enviro-humor: How does a Buddhist order a hot dog? Make me one with everything.

———

The removal of the trees and fish of the Archipelago in ignorance of their true value to the system of life into which they are woven is not without precedent, that's for sure. We humans have limped along with oversimplified notions about taking what we call "natural resources" from places like the Tongass chiefly because we perceive ourselves at the center of the consumptive cycle. We are also impeded in our judgment by the human life span, less than a hundred years, and economic systems which contain no real long-range vision. Only in the last quarter of this century have we begun to understand that this old-growth forest has far more value than the dollars contained in top-grade wood products and the cosmetic charm of the tourist business. The forests also purify water, store carbon, and enable salmon, bears, humans, wolves, birds, deer, insects, worms, and countless plants and creatures to exist. In a complex relationship with all other life, the trees stabilize the giant organism we call the earth. Salmon have helped to deliver the news.

They have been food for as long as other critters have been around to eat them, and human myths, ceremonies, and respect have been engendered as much by gratitude for a meal as by appreciation for their enigmatic spirits. Pacific salmon are anadromous—the word means "up-running." They are born in fresh water, migrate to the sea to mature, return to fresh water, and spawn. (Catadromous is the opposite, meaning down running like most eels that return to the sea to spawn.) All salmon but the steelhead are semelparous. (A fish that dies after spawning once is semelparous.) Atlantic salmon, of the genus *Salmo*, are anadromous but not semelparous, and steelhead, too, spawn more than once.

A classic example of ordering-a-hot-dog wisdom links fish to rocks to trees. Salmon probably became anadromous to adapt to the cycles of ice and water that have dominated their range since the Pleistocene when they evolved to their present form in the cold, nutrient-poor fresh water of northern latitudes. From time to time, great glaciers completely hushed the continental rivers and lakes beneath crackling blankets of ice, and drove the fish to sea. Salmon are among the quickest studies in the evolutionary drama, able to change so rapidly in just a few generations that geneticists favor them for experiments in mutation and adaptation. They evolved the physiological and biochemical traits necessary to migration, homing, and survival in both fresh and salt water, and further refined themselves into hundreds of races distinctly bound to specific watersheds. Every salmon is a member of not only its broad taxonomic species like king or coho, but of a natal subgroup from their particular stream or river, marked by distinct traits such as scale color, size, flesh color, and even taste to a predator.

Georg Steller, the legendary German naturalist who sailed to within a few hundred miles of the Tongass with Vitus Bering on his second voyage to North America in 1741–42, was the first to list the species of Pacific salmon. The names he gave them are Russian in origin because Steller and Bering were on the Tsar's payroll. Fifty years later, Johann Julius Wilbaum, a German ichthyologist, used Steller's notes to formally describe the members of the genus *Oncorhynchus*: *O. tsawytscha* (chinook); *O. kisutch* (coho); *O. nerka* (sockeye); *O. keta* (chum); *O. gorbuscha* (pink); and *O. masou* (cherry). Later, we described *O. Amago* and *O. mykiss* (steelhead). We know them, too, by the seasons of their return, and the names of the rivers and tributaries to which they are bound as surely as red blood cells in arteries, veins, and capillaries. A king salmon is a king salmon, but a king from the outer watersheds of Prince of Wales Island is subtly but clearly a salmon with a different accent than a king from an Admiralty Island drainage on Chatham Strait.

Each species, and in some cases each race or run within a species, carries a schedule for fresh and salt water migration in its genetic code. All five species of salmon that spawn in North American rivers are represented in the Tongass.

Chinook salmon, adapted to long or steep rivers, build strength and size during as many as five years at sea after a year in fresh water. A seiner off Prince of Wales Island caught a 145-pounder, though surely bigger chinooks have lived and live now.

The coho's anadromous rhythm is similar to chinook's, its closest relative, though their sea time is shorter, usually only eighteen months or two years. If salmon were automobiles, cohos would be sports cars, fast, agile, and compact. The biggest ones, late in the season when all the fattening is done, can weigh 20 pounds.

The annual cycles of the sockeye are the most varied of the tribe, from a few weeks to three years in fresh water, and from one to four years in the sea. Their life spans are so varied because they depend on more ecological combinations, patterns, and sizes of lakes, streams, and rivers than any other salmon. Some biologists spend their entire careers on the complicated sockeye, trying to predict the timing and size of the runs for commercial packers who want to know how much money to borrow to finance their seasons, and how much to pay the fishermen who always think it's not enough. (The kokanee, a close cousin of the sockeye, has even abandoned its anadromous instincts in favor of life as a smaller fish in landlocked lakes.)

Chums are the blue-collar salmon, dependable, nothing fancy, the most widely distributed of all species, once ranging from Korea around the Pacific Rim to Monterey Bay, California. Second only to chinooks in size, the worker-like chums usually return in two waves, summer and late fall when they are the last of the salmon to reach their home rivers. They leave their streams within months of spawning, and return with a territorial precision notable even among salmon after two to five years at sea.

Pinks, by comparison, are zoom salmon. After just a few months in fresh water and a single winter at sea, they return in great swarms of three- to six-pound fish. Throughout their range from the Sea of Japan to the Sacramento River, "humpies" spawn in alternating big and small years, and we know why. Because of their short life cycles, each year's pink salmon never mix with another's, so runs in odd- and even-numbered years have become genetically isolated and radically different in size.

Until 1992, steelhead were included in the *Salmo* tribe, but taxonomists reclassified the species as *O. mykiss*, true Pacific salmon. They are the only members of the *Oncorhynchus* tribe that make whoopee more than once. Masu and Amago occur only in Asian watersheds, and for most of our history with salmon have been considered a single species. Each has a close cousin that has not evolved an anadromous life cycle and remains exclusively in fresh water. They spend one or more years in their rivers, a winter in the ocean, and spawn in early fall after a full summer back in their rivers. In Japanese, these gold and silver salmon are sakuramasu, which means "cherry trout" because they return to the river at about the same time the cherry blossoms signal spring's arrival.

All Pacific salmon share common patterns of emergence, maturation, and reproduction that bind them to their streams and shape them for survival in the ocean. Chief among the survival mechanisms of the species is sheer abundance, since going the distance from egg to spawner is a numbers game. Ask anyone who's spent a summer on a counting tower. If S is the number of salmon that must return to perpetuate a healthy run, thousands of times S must be fertilized eggs. (My numbers are not scientific fact, but comparisons of magnitude that vary for each species.) Hundreds of times S must survive the delicate emergence into alevin, flashing bits of protein becoming living creatures in full view.

These transparent, eyed beings hunker down in the substrate of their natal streams and feed off their own egg sacs during the still months of winter and early spring when predators are likely to leave them be. Then, still hundreds of times S must survive to become fry, real fish with their egg sacs consumed, their bodies zipped up, fins, and tails. As juveniles or smolt, the new fish begin actively eating and being eaten. Herons, gulls, eagles, osprey, and other birds thin their numbers as the salmon work their way downstream to the sea, and seals, sea lions, otters, and bigger fish wait hungrily in the estuaries. On most rivers at the end of the twentieth century, the salmon are also put in dire straits by logging that trashes their spawning habitat, pollution, dams, and urban sprawl. Once in the sea, predators, including fishermen, claim their shares of the salmon runs, further reducing S until, finally, the survivors reach home to spawn. Though their powers of navigation are studied and celebrated, it is probably their genetic programming that allows a few to stray in every run. That way, they can survive the natural destruction of their spawning streams by ice, floods, and fire. They are, sadly, having trouble adjusting to the chain saw.

The earliest treaties, agreements, and conciliations among the people of the Pacific Rim sorted out rights to salmon, first as matters of tradition, then as matters of law, but always because salmon are vital as food. The Tlingit and Haida people of the ancient Tongass watersheds defined their band and family relationships according to ancestral rights to particular streams and salmon runs. Only in the 1950s were those fishing rights officially abrogated by the courts of the United States as part of the first land settlement between the early people and the recently arrived Americans. By that time, the industrial fleets and packers were in full flower, migrating north each year to take advantage of the last thriving salmon runs on the planet. By mid-century, they had been through total collapse and renewal several times because they did not live in the watersheds they plundered.

For thousands of years in the human relationship with salmon, though, nobody trapped, caught, or ate anything anonymously. The links between water, fish, trees, and people were not scientifically defined, but they were perfectly clear and understood in taboos and traditions. Commerce in distant markets and cash economies broke those instinctive bonds forever, and replaced them with the impersonal networks of industrial fishing, canning, and freezing. Now, salmon reach tables around the world but most carry no ecological return address. Stewardship has proven impossible at a distance.

Habitat is where it's at. To modern people, dams, timber, and great cities were part of the vision of paradise, engineers were priests, and the forces of nature mere puzzles with certain solutions. Coastal and watershed destruction to encourage commerce is not an aberration of industrial culture but a definitive characteristic, and no nation can claim restraint on behalf of salmon. Even today, as the somber notes of acute ecosystem crisis are sounding on dozens of North American watersheds, cavalier politicians support destructive logging and mining practices in Alaska and British Columbia, assuring us that they will not harm the few healthy salmon runs that are left.

Whether motivated by long-range vision or short-term greed, the people of the Pacific tacitly agree to the bargain that is killing off salmon. Millions of other people in Asia and Europe are already paying the true price for similar alterations in their relationships with the habitat of Pacific and Atlantic salmon. The mainland drainages of the Tumen, Amur, Anadyr, Markova, Elbe, Danube, Rhine, Thames, Spey, Hudson, and Connecticut Rivers and the numberless shorter watercourses of the Newfoundland, Kurile, and Japanese archipelagos once were graced by salmon every year. As miner's canaries for the health of watersheds, salmon carry a message of distress by their absence. A salmon watershed without salmon is no longer singing the song of life. Until recently, early and modern people relied upon super-abundance and their ability to move on if they overfished a salmon run, or trashed a stream or other life-support systems. Alaska, including the fragile watersheds of the Tongass, is the last place to run to.

Putting up Pacific salmon on an industrial scale began in 1864 on the Sacramento River when the Hume brothers—William, George, Robert, and Joseph—arrived with a tinsmith, Andrew Hapgood.

Sixty years before they came west, Nicolas Appert, a vintner, beer maker, and chef had invented the canning process and won Napoleon Bonaparte's 1,200-franc prize for coming up with a way to feed advancing armies. Subsequent refinements in the process eliminated some of the spoilage that plagued canners and armies, tin cans replaced glass jars, and, finally, Pasteur tied bacteria to disease. Not incidentally, he figured out why food rotted and what to do about it. In 1840, the first canned salmon in North America was packed on the Bay of Fundy, not too far north of Maine, the childhood home of the Humes and Hapgood.

At first, the packers cut out their cans with tin snips, soldered them by hand, filled each with the very tasty, very expensive salmon that was worth about $1 a can in England, crimped and soldered tops, and submitted the miraculous package to heat in a retort. A good tinsmith could make a hundred cans a day, and an entire year's pack was less than 100,000 cans. Trapping the salmon in the river was easy and cheap, so in short order, Hapgood and Hume got rich and expanded into real canneries from their family shed. Markets for salmon that would keep for more than a week seemed endless and the rush was on, every bit the equal of any attack of gold fever.

In a few years, a combination of salmon lust on the Sacramento and hydrologic mining, a particularly virulent method that blasted enormous quantities of mud and gravel into the rivers and streams, had just about wiped out the runs and spawning beds in that watershed. So the salmon canners spread north, first to the Rogue River, then the Columbia, the Fraser, and the smaller watercourses in between. Competitors challenged Hume and Hapgood, and eventually, fleets of square riggers sailed for Alaskan waters. As the years ticked over into the American Century, the unbridled canners were packing salmon on every spawning river from California to the Arctic Circle, and canned salmon began its eighty-year run as a staple food. From 1870 to 1950, you could open ten cupboards anywhere in Europe or North America and probably find a can of salmon in seven of them.

Though salmon traps and weirs were the mainstays of hundreds of chugging canneries, eventually men in boats had to venture away from the rivers into the sea to supply the packing lines. What we now celebrate as commercial salmon fishing arrived on the Pacific. Every spring, full-rigged ships sailed north from San Francisco to Southeast Alaska, across the Gulf, west along the Aleutians, through Unimak Pass and into the Bering Sea. The Alaska fleet was the last hurrah for the square riggers, including *Star of India, Abner Coburn, Benjamin F. Packard,* and *Glory of the Seas.* The shorter voyage and supply lines to Southeast Alaska produced permanent canneries and herring reduction plants in virtually every cove and bay in the Tongass. Not until the 1920s, when many of the once vigorous runs of Bristol Bay and Southeast Alaska became pathetic trickles, did anyone give much thought to restraint. The legacy of this excess fell to the local fishermen, who eventually succeeded in wresting much of the power from the packers at statehood. Alaskans banned traps and eventually placed the rights to the fish in the hands of the fishermen by limiting entry to the grounds. The fleets were under control, but until the ecological renaissance of the Eighties and Nineties, salmon and timber were commodities to be extracted, their worth computed by the pound and board foot. Our understanding of the complex dependencies of the rainforest is still incomplete and we finally suspect that we are living incompetently, that we have evolved unnatural relationships with our food, shelter, and water. The feedback loop of excess and consequence is closing, though, and we are once again, as were early people, realizing that we cut no tree and catch no fish anonymously.

For a short time, I fished for a living under the apparently simple terms of anonymous extraction. It was a wonderful life. One night in a bar in Sitka, another fisherman pointed that trolling for salmon in Southeast Alaska is one of the last best things a self-indulgent liberal arts major can do for a living. The Pioneer is to commercial fishing what Sardi's is to the theater in New York, a big, warm bar room with black-and-white photographs of fishing boats and fishing people instead of stage celebrities covering every inch of the walls. In a meandering but eloquent monologue, my friend argued that literature and history, along with a fear of real jobs, prepared us for hard, dangerous work on small boats, rewarded by great beauty and just enough money to pay the bills.

But even before my friend delivered his inspired vision on that well-lubricated night, I knew that I would have gone fishing for nothing. The water, the forest, the people, and the salmon of the Archipelago were enough to claim me. Trollers often fish alone, catch salmon one at a time on hooks, and depend entirely upon guile, instinct, sham, trickery, and luck for success. The kings and cohos we hunted traveled thousands of miles to complete the circles of their lives in the streams they inherited from the previous generation. They are wondrous creatures that have been around for millions of years, track the magnetic field of the earth to navigate, and return carrying nutrients from the deep sea to their ancestral watersheds. Though I was paid to catch them to feed people all over the world, fishing for salmon was anything but a job.

Trolling in Southeast Alaska was this: I am at anchor in the lee of Point Adolphus, an idyllic promontory on the north end of Chichagof Island, directly across Icy Strait from Glacier Bay. There, the Pacific invades the northern reaches of the archipelago through a gap just a few hundred yards wide and at speeds of up to eight knots, and encounters its first major terrestrial obstacle. When the current peaks, the collision churns the water into a symphony of feeding fish, birds, seals, whales, and porpoise. Fishing, therefore, was often great, especially when accompanied by the primitive pleasure of knowing that I was just another creature clinging to the very visible marine food web.

The sensory snapshots of that morning evoke fish, water, and trees. The ocean roars and swells, gathering itself into rips and maelstroms of astonishing power, while swarms of thrashing needlefish, herring, and salmon stipple the surface. Synchronized swarms of northern phalaropes flash alternately brown and white, as though to the tapping toe of an invisible choreographer who occasionally orders them from the sky into undulating rafts on the chrome-black water. Beyond the phalaropes, a few miles across the strait through clearing tendrils of fog, are the peaks of the Fairweather Range and the icy uplands of Glacier Bay. The rivers of ice are remnants of the thick skin of frozen water that as recently as 14,000 years ago covered not only the strait where I lay at anchor but all the entire hemisphere north to the pole and south to the latitude of Puget Sound.

As I sip my coffee on deck, the water itself enchants me, there on display in its three astonishing states, liquid, gas, and solid. Water is odorless, colorless, and tasteless, a compound of enormous stability and a powerful solvent that is repelled by most organic substances but attracted by inorganic materials including itself. Water expands when frozen, rather than contracting like most substances, so the solid is lighter than the liquid, which, of course, is why ice floats. If water suddenly started behaving like almost every other molecule and weighed more frozen than as a liquid, life as we know it would depart. Ice would sink to the bottom of the oceans and the summer sun would not be strong enough to melt it at such great depths. Life in the water would cease, the seas would disappear, the hydrologic cycle upon which our existence is based would grind to a halt. Our food is not only mostly water, but utterly dependent on it; a one-pound loaf of bread has used up about two tons of water while the wheat was growing. A salmon needs the water of an ocean, a stream, and a forest to grow.

I remember that morning at Point Adolphus like a poker player remembers a pat hand because the sensual feast kindled a new awareness of the bonds between the water, forest, and salmon of the Tongass. By the time Jim Baichtel put salmon in the trees for me at that potluck in Ketchikan, most fishermen in Southeast had caught on, too, and joined ranks with environmental advocates and other outraged citizens to force reform of logging practices. Unfortunately, trees and a salmon are still commodities to be consumed, rather than deeply connected parts of the same whole, and separating them in the minds of people who eat and use them remains a disservice to all. The jobs vs. the environment paradigm continues to corrupt our political solutions to abusive logging. And at the fish market, you can buy farmed salmon from pens instead of streams and the sea, further relieving consumers of the demand for stewardship. Maybe we'd get the picture if each farmed salmon carried the brutal truth in a cigarette-like caveat: "This salmon cannot spawn in trees and may be hazardous to your health."

CPSIA information can be obtained at www.ICGtesting.com
Printed in the USA
BVOW081133270712

296238BV00004B/3/P